The Theatre of Albert Camus
A Critical Study

The Theatre of Albert Camus

A Critical Study

E. FREEMAN

METHUEN & CO LTD
11 New Fetter Lane London EC4

First published in 1971
by Methuen & Co Ltd
11 New Fetter Lane, London EC4
© 1971 E. Freeman
Printed in Great Britain by
The Camelot Press Ltd
London and Southampton

SBN 416 12940 4

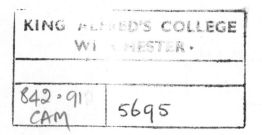
Distributed in the USA
by Barnes & Noble Inc

Contents

Acknowledgements

For their helpful replies to my queries about Camus's work and its sources I wish to thank Mmes G. Brée and S. Agnely, and Messrs R. Quilliot, J. Grenier, R. Char, R. Gay-Crosier, A. Anglès, J. P. V. D. Balsdon, E. O. Marsh and P. Thody.

I am particularly indebted to Professor W. D. Howarth, Dr K. Gore and Dr M. Thomas for their extremely valuable aid and advice at various times during the preparation of this book.

Grateful acknowledgement is due to the editors of *Forum for Modern Language Studies*, *Symposium* and *Modern Language Quarterly* for permission to quote material first published in those journals, and to Chatto and Windus Ltd for permission to quote from William Faulkner's *Requiem for a Nun* and from David Magarshack's translation of Dostoevsky's *The Devils*.

All references to Camus's works, with the exception of his notebooks (*Carnets*), are based on the two Pléiade volumes edited by Roger Quilliot:

Vol. 1, *Théâtre, Récits, Nouvelles* (Paris, Gallimard, 1962).

Referred to as *TRN* in notes.

Vol. 2, *Essais* (Paris, Gallimard, 1965; Quilliot assisted by L. Faucon).

Referred to as *Essais* in notes.

Camus's *Carnets*, however, are published separately by Gallimard; Vol. 1 (covering 1935–42) in 1962, and Vol. 2 (1942–51) in 1964.

1 The Background

Je préfère la compagnie des gens de théâtre, vertueux ou pas, à celle des intellectuels, mes frères.

Albert Camus, 'Pourquoi je fais du théâtre'

The renaissance of the French theatre in the middle of the twentieth century stands out sharply against the sombre background of contemporary European civilization. In the decade before the First World War the French theatre was at its lowest ebb. Twenty-five years later, on the eve of the Second World War, it was in the process of becoming better than it had ever been since the seventeenth century. Between 1930 and 1960, and more particularly during the decade of the forties, Paris witnessed a flowering of talents which produced a body of dramatic literature unsurpassed in theatrical brilliance and philosophical insight since the work of the great trio of the Classical French theatre, Corneille, Molière and Racine. During the 250 years which had elapsed since that great age only three French dramatists of outstanding and durable merit had emerged: Marivaux, Beaumarchais and Musset. But these were isolated and unconnected explosions of genius. Now all of a sudden nearly a dozen great dramatists appeared at the same time and for at least a decade won for the theatre the leading position among the arts in France. This book is an attempt to assess the place of Albert Camus in that renaissance. In time will the man who was regarded in 1945 as one of the great hopes of the French theatre in fact rank alongside Claudel, Giraudoux, Anouilh, Montherlant, Sartre, Ionesco, Beckett and Genet? How much did Camus contribute, either in theory or in practice, to the modern movement, and how lasting do his plays appear to be some ten years after his premature death in 1960?

Many who are interested in modern French literature, particularly in the English-speaking world, know Camus mainly if not exclusively as a novelist and philosopher. The Frenchman who in 1957, at the early age of forty-four, was awarded the Nobel Prize for Literature, was known as the author of the novels *L'Étranger*, *La Peste* and *La Chute*, and of the philosophical essays *Le Mythe de Sisyphe* and *L'Homme révolté*. His theatre is usually considered to be a marginal activity, to be tucked away conveniently in one chapter near the end of critical studies of his work. In fact Albert Camus was an actor and director of no mean competence who wrote, adapted or translated more than a dozen plays and was devoted to the theatre throughout his life. From 1935 to 1959 it was his first and his last form of artistic expression. A majority of the leading French writers of this century have achieved some degree of success in both the major media, prose fiction and the theatre. More often than not it is a case of a writer turning to the theatre after first expressing himself in the novel: Gide, Cocteau, Bernanos, Green, Mauriac, Sartre, Simone de Beauvoir and Beckett are the best examples. Camus stands out from the great contemporary novelist-playwrights not only through having been a playwright from his earliest years as a writer but through having a far greater connection with the professional theatre than any of them, and perhaps even more than playwrights such as Anouilh and Ionesco who have devoted themselves almost exclusively to the medium.

Throughout his life Camus experienced profound satisfaction when working in any capacity in the theatre. Acting or directing gave him the opportunity to know that sense of exaltation which springs from sharing a task with a small, dedicated band of people in whom complete trust can be placed. He compared the experience on various occasions to the feeling of *solidarité* and total commitment which he enjoyed in activities as diverse as fighting in the Resistance and playing soccer (he played in goal for Algiers University when a student and was a fan throughout his life). He once stated that the soccer field and the theatre were the two places in the world where he felt happy and at ease. A personable and handsome man, and a good mimic, Camus enjoyed the company of actors (and actresses!) and theatre people in general, and made no secret of the fact that he would have been quite content to make his living as an actor or director. It is significant that although Camus was frequently the object of bitter recrimination because of his political and philosophical views he could nevertheless count on the unending loyalty of the people who worked with him in the theatre, even after failures as resounding as that of *L'État de siège*, his highly ambitious venture with Jean-Louis Barrault in 1948. When, after Camus's death in a motor accident in 1960, tributes flooded in from eminent figures in many different spheres of public life, the most authentic and deeply felt were those which testified to his skill and sensitivity as a director and to the sincerity with which he devoted himself to his productions and his casts.

Above all, and more than for social and psychological reasons, Camus devoted himself to the theatre throughout his life because he believed it to be the greatest form of artistic expression. In the age of Pericles and during the Renaissance the theatre was the centre of civilized existence to which the greatest talents applied themselves. Camus sincerely hoped that this state of affairs might repeat itself in his lifetime. He hoped particularly that the greatest type of theatre – tragedy – might be re-created in a modern form. His own original plays and some of his adaptations thus represent the effort made by one of the leading French writers of the twentieth century to revive great and tragic theatre after an interval of nearly 300 years. For Camus, as for the many other European or American playwrights who have been engaged in this quest in recent times, two considerable difficulties had to be tackled. First, the necessity of finding a mythic theme in an age which lacks a fundamental religious sense of awe. Almost every one of Camus's great contemporary French dramatists turned to the Greeks at least once, and used the myths of Antigone, Oedipus, Orestes, Electra and the Trojan War to incarnate the political and metaphysical dilemmas of the twentieth century. Camus was hostile to this trend.[1] Nor did he favour using historical and legendary material from the Middle Ages and Renaissance. His theatre is a search for a modern myth made significant for contemporary audiences, not by reviving Joan of Arc, Christopher Columbus or Inès de Castro, but by creating heroes embodying the dilemmas of ordinary men in the twentieth century. The second problem was that of style, which Camus considered to be of the greatest importance. With one or two rare exceptions no one had used the classical French verse form, the alexandrine, as a medium for serious and heroic theatre since the Romantic era. On the other hand many of Camus's contemporaries went to the opposite extreme: naturalistic dialogue recording the speech patterns of modern French with an almost electronic fidelity. Camus's four original plays are an attempt at finding a compromise: a stylized, polished dialogue sufficiently remote to evoke an aura of classical solemnity and yet both familiar and articulate enough to be relevant to contemporary man and the philosophical complexity of his problems.

Camus's career in the theatre may be divided into three distinct, major phases: 1935–9; 1944–9; 1950–60. The first of these was his period of dramatic apprenticeship in Algeria. This was when Camus learned to act, direct and write the hard way – and some would say the best way – by putting on plays in hazardous economic circumstances, picking up the tricks of the trade through repertory work and participating in all aspects of production: painting sets one minute and acting Ivan Karamazov the next. Technically, Camus, as virtually the sole animator of *avant-garde* theatre in Algeria at this time, was very experimental and fully alive to current trends in European theatre. At the very beginning of this phase Camus was a Communist, and not unnaturally influenced by some of the epic and agit-prop techniques of Brecht and Piscator, a style which, like the associated ideology, he soon came to regard as a false start to his career.[2] More significant by the end of this period is the effect of perhaps the two most influential Frenchmen in twentieth-century French theatre, Jacques Copeau and Antonin Artaud. Significant because Copeau re-oriented the professional theatre towards the highest aesthetic and philosophical standards; and Artaud claimed for it in

Le Théâtre et son double (1938) a revolutionary, metaphysical function, that of shocking the spectator into a re-examination of his whole being, by means of a catharsis more total than anything envisaged by Aristotle.

The second phase, 1944–9, is the high-water mark of Camus's dramatic activity. This is the period during which his four original plays, *Caligula, Le Malentendu, L'État de siège* and *Les Justes,* were all given fully professional Paris productions, in most cases calling on the best talents available in the French theatre. This was one of the most exciting and dynamic times in French theatre history, one during which Claudel, Cocteau, Anouilh, Giraudoux and Salacrou, whose pre-war reputations were consolidated, were joined or succeeded by Camus, Sartre and Montherlant. This was the time when Camus's twin philosophical themes found their expression in the theatre: the absurd and revolt. In his highly original essay, *Le Mythe de Sisyphe,* published at the beginning of the war, Camus formulated what was implicit in the work he had already published: life is *absurd,* incoherent, resistant to scrutiny, almost perverse in its working. Man's traditional reaction to this discovery, according to Camus, has been suicide, either literally physical suicide or 'philosophical' suicide – flight into the solace of religion, the blind leap of faith. Camus now advocated in *Le Mythe de Sisyphe* a third solution. Man who becomes aware of the absurd should not capitulate by either of these two traditional reactions to the spiritual tension, but rather should try to maintain it. He should retain a courageous lucidity in the face of ultimate meaninglessness and the certainty and finality of death. For the fact that life has no meaning does not mean that it is not worth living. On the contrary, *absurd man,* shorn of any illusions about the possibility of a physical or transcendental Utopia, can be spurred on to the greater enjoyment of the here and now. Despair, if contained, may lead paradoxically to a stoic exaltation, even joy.

Camus's four plays are all based on the premiss that life is absurd, although with varying degrees of explicitness. The first two, *Caligula* and *Le Malentendu,* dwell mainly on the meta-physical and abstract nature of the absurd. The last two, *L'État de*

5

siège and *Les Justes*, written some five years later, by which time Camus had lost all of his illusions about what might be achieved in post-war France, concentrate more on its social and political consequences. All four plays, however, part company with *Le Mythe de Sisyphe* in an important way. The possibility of a fourth type of reaction to the discovery of the absurd is a vital element of the plot and characterization, if not the sole dynamic. Each play contains at least one major character who is unable to preserve the tension of the absurd and whose initial instinct is to commit homicide rather than suicide (and is reduced to suicide in the end). Stoic self-containment is abandoned. The 'absurd man' attempts to become the ally and propagator of the absurd, rather than its victim. From 1945 onwards Camus associated this philosophical reaction more and more explicitly with the ruthlessness and fanaticism of twentieth-century totalitarianism, particularly Stalinism, and said as much in his long and controversial essay *L'Homme révolté*, published in 1951. *L'État de siège* and *Les Justes* are vitally linked to this work with its thesis that since the French Revolution humanitarian ideologies have been betrayed every time *revolt* ('la révolte métaphysique') has turned into *revolution* ('la révolte historique'). With their political commitment and didacticism, the two plays are fundamentally different from *Caligula* and *Le Malentendu* in their artistic approach. It is important to note, however, that even the two last-named plays are based on the distinction between revolt and revolution, although with no overt political reference. Attempts have occasionally been made to categorize Camus's plays by saying that the first two are plays about the absurd, and the last two, *L'État de siège* and *Les Justes*, are about revolt. This is quite misleading, since all four plays are in some measure based on the premiss that life is absurd and examine the two possible reactions to it, revolt and revolution. The difference between the plays depends upon the balance of emphasis in each case, particularly the fact that in his last two plays Camus applies a specifically political and historical meaning to 'revolution'.

Camus's writing took an increasingly moralistic turn in the

late 1940s. The culmination of his polemics against revolutionary and totalitarian ideology was *L'Homme révolté* which created a furore and a break with many of his friends on the extreme left of French politics. By one of those well-known political processes of asserting that anyone who is not 100 per cent with you is by definition your enemy, they argued that Camus the courageous editor of the clandestine Resistance newspaper *Combat*, the passionate anti-Fascist and anti-Nazi, was no more. He had defected to the right. The result of these allegations was a personal and artistic crisis from which Camus never fully recovered. During the last ten years of his life he contented himself with translating and/or adapting six works for the theatre. Two of these were novels, Faulkner's *Requiem for a Nun* and Dostoevsky's *The Devils*. The latter, presenting immense technical problems and contrasting with Faulkner's novel which already has a unique dramatic form, was the nearest Camus came to writing anything original for the theatre during the whole of this period. This third and last phase of his career in the theatre was one during which, perhaps for somewhat therapeutic reasons, Camus did much the same sort of thing that he had done as a young man in Algeria. He was now able to work much more actively in the theatre than he had during the 1945–9 phase, doing a certain amount of directing, experimenting in theatrical styles, and, some think, preparing for a creative come-back.

Most of this book is quite naturally given over to the central phase of Camus's career, and a chapter is devoted to each of his four original plays. I have related the theme of each play to the novels and philosophical essays where relevant, but above all attempted to appraise Camus's theatre *as theatre* rather than as philosophical literature which just happens to be in dramatic form. This central material is framed by two chapters covering the first and last phases of Camus's activity. Throughout I have attached importance to Camus's search for a personal dramatic style, and tried to pick out the essential characteristics of the dialogue and dramatic structure of his plays. In this particular respect (and independently of their philosophical significance) *Requiem pour une nonne* and *Les Possédés* are of greater interest from a technical point of view than is commonly realized, since they show us Camus making plays not *ex nihilo* but by selecting, rejecting and altering the substance of novels which, each in very different ways, already contain much dialogue and inherent dramatic material.

At the same time I have cross-referred frequently to Camus's contemporaries and suggested ways in which he resembles or differs from the other great dramatists of the modern movement. It is possible to distinguish a number of important developments in the French theatre from about 1930 onwards. To begin with, as a result mainly of the dedication and courage of the great critic and director Jacques Copeau at the beginning of the century, the French theatre acquired a far greater integrity than it had ever had previously. Before the First World War ninety per cent or more of the French theatre (and that meant Parisian much more than it does now) was an entirely commercial affair. The controlling force was the owners and managers of the 'boulevard' theatres in the smart Right-Bank areas of Paris. Playwrights existed to provide scripts which would cater for the physical and histrionic talents of star actresses and actors. Scripts were preferably daring without being intellectually demanding of performer or spectator, hence Henri Bataille's *La Femme nue*, *La Vierge folle* and *Le Scandale*. Somewhere near the bottom of the hierarchy was the director, whose job it was to show off the stars to best advantage, and see that they turned up for rehearsals as often as possible and learnt their lines more or less accurately, give or take a bit of leeway during the obligatory tirades; above all he had to make sure that they did not walk out of the show as that would cost him his job and the management a lot of money.

Copeau changed much of this, directly or indirectly. By the time the young Camus was coming into the theatre in the late 1930s the spirit of the French theatre had been transformed by a generation of dedicated and inspired directors who were Copeau's contemporaries or disciples: Lugné-Poe, Pitoëff, Dullin, Baty, Gémier, Jouvet. These were all men who, although frequently conflicting in their styles, were united in regarding the theatre as

8

an art rather than a business, and an art which could be both experimental and popular. Like the team which Copeau trained when he founded his famous Théâtre du Vieux-Colombier on the Left Bank in 1913, actors were now expected to be disciplined, versatile, skilled in all the theatre arts, and subordinated to the overall interests of the production. Above all, a far more responsible and artistically sophisticated attitude now prevailed in all quarters, among critics, playwrights, performers and public. The various types of play against which Copeau inveighed so passionately during the *belle époque* – frothy, (extra-)marital farces or urbane bourgeois dramas with well-contrived plots and characterization – were now seen for what they were: third-rate efforts aimed at the box-office. They were not wiped out, nor will they ever be. Nor was the personality cult of the star. But at least the competition to this sort of theatre was much more powerful than that which had existed during Copeau's early days, when little more than token resistance was offered by the isolated and esoteric *avant-garde* extremes of naturalism (Antoine) and symbolism (Lugné-Poe and Paul Fort). Now, during Camus's formative years, the French theatre benefited from a number of stylish and authentic productions of the French and ancient Greek classics, Shakespeare and Calderón, and was increasingly receptive to the work of French dramatists who had something to say and a genuinely theatrical style in which to say it. In this respect one can hardly over-stress the inspiration provided by the great contemporary Italian dramatist Luigi Pirandello, the sensational success of whose *Six Characters in Search of an Author* in Paris in 1923 is a landmark in the history of the French theatre. In this and many other plays which were performed in Paris in the 1920s and 1930s Pirandello put over a message of tragic profundity by means of spectacular and ingenious techniques of characterization and structure: the manipulation of illusion and truth, the mask and the face, the play within a play.

Of course, the new French dramatists did not break with the boulevard completely. Cocteau, Giraudoux and the latter's director, Jouvet, had a healthy respect for the box-office, as did

Anouilh, whose plays, furthermore, are just as 'well-made' as any by Scribe and Sardou in the nineteenth century. Montherlant's plays depend heavily on complex psychology; Sartre is not averse to an old-fashioned *coup de théâtre*, and bourgeois family conflicts and sexual entanglements are not uncommon in all these dramatists. And one of the principal criticisms of Camus which I shall examine in detail is that, whatever he said in theory, he lacked in practice the true Copeau sense of the theatrical experience – a well-harmonized synthesis of plastic and literary art – and that his theatre is first and foremost a theatre of debate, just like that of Dumas *fils* and Augier. It is of far greater literary merit, of course, and far subtler in the themes it debates, but every bit as dependent on words *and words alone* as the work of the earnest moralizers whom Copeau denounced at the beginning of the century.

And yet there is an important difference in the work of the dramatists who came to the fore in the 1930s and 1940s. These elements of the boulevard theatre are essentially borrowings which are carefully integrated into the artistic whole. Exacerbated sexuality, morbid psychology, the class system or ingenious theatricality for its own sake are not the *raison d'être* of this movement, despite what, because of one or other of these factors, Camus himself said about Giraudoux, and what some feel about Sartre and many about Anouilh. If Sartre's *Les Mains sales*, Anouilh's *Antigone* and Montherlant's *Le Maître de Santiago* are compelling theatre of a kind not seen before on the French stage it is because the qualities of the characterization and dramatic structure are accompanied by something which is lacking in the work of the adroit manipulators of plot and character from Dumas *fils* to Bernstein: a metaphysical dimension. To appreciate the greatness of the French dramatists who reached their maturity during the Second World War it is of course important not to be put off by plays like Anouilh's *La Sauvage* and *L'Hermine* and Sartre's *La Putain respectueuse* and *Nekrassov*. In their best work – and that is what every artist has the right to be judged by – Sartre, Anouilh, Camus and Montherlant create characters whom the psychoanalyst and the sociologist can probe only superficially before in the last resort coming up against the impenetrable wall of the absurd. For these are essentially symbolic heroes representing Western humanist values in conflict with overwhelming destructive forces. It was the approaching shadow of the Second World War which impressed the fundamental absurdity of existence and the inadequacy of traditional solutions on the mature Giraudoux and young writers like Anouilh, Sartre and the Camus who was in the process of drafting *Caligula*. Violence and horror, the inevitability and finality of death, the vertiginous isolation of man forced to take extreme actions: these became the themes of the French theatre of the 1940s. It is fitting that it was via the unique communal experience of the theatre, and sometimes by means of the same sort of classical and national myths which embodied Greek and Renaissance tragedy, that the French tried to give meaning and form to the shapeless mass of despair and confusion which was their common lot at this time.

2 Apprenticeship: *Révolte dans les Asturies*

Le théâtre n'est pas un jeu, c'est là ma conviction.

Camus

Camus was born on 7 November 1913 in Mondovi, Algeria, into a family of working-class European settlers. His father, Lucien Camus, descended from the wave of French emigrants who left Alsace after the Franco-Prussian War, was killed in 1914 in the battle of the Marne. Mme Camus, *née* Catherine Sintès, of Spanish descent, immediately moved to the working-class district of Belcourt in Algiers. Here, with her two infant sons and other relatives, she had a difficult existence. Of his early years Camus was later to say: 'je n'ai pas appris la liberté dans Marx. Il est vrai: je l'ai apprise dans la misère.' Or, as Joseph Levine, with admirable Jewish irony, said of his own childhood: 'A tenement. The usual bit: with the rats and a stepfather.' In Camus's case it was cockroaches and a grandmother armed with a whip.

Those who favour a certain kind of environmental approach may scan Camus's childhood in vain for signs of the future devotee of the theatre: no playlets written to amuse his friends, no comfortable middle-class *sorties* on Thursday afternoons to see the French classics, no parent (such as Anouilh's) who was once an *artiste* at Arcachon. His answer to Carl Viggiani's question: 'Avez-vous fait du théâtre au lycée?' was quite simply 'Non, je faisais du football.' Camus in fact enjoyed a rough-and-tumble childhood, characterized by an almost total cultural deprivation in his home background, brought up as he was by a tyrannical grandmother and a deaf, overworked, widowed mother who had little education and seldom spoke. The silent, inaccessible mother-figure, too exhausted to manifest the affection that her sons needed, was to be evoked not without emotion by Camus in one of his first essays,

'Entre oui et non', in the collection *L'Envers et l'endroit* of 1937, and reappeared in Camus's mature work, notably in his play *Le Malentendu*.

This environment of poverty, if not of out-and-out squalor, and this lack of early exposure to the theatre, may perhaps account for certain features of Camus's dramatic style. His theory and practice were to be characterized by a certain degree of what one can only call puritanism in respect of both form and content. For social as much as for artistic reasons, Camus was to abhor the *belle époque* tradition with all its boulevard trappings, catering for a predominantly middle-class, Parisian public requiring a few hours of star-spangled titillation between restaurant and bed. At the same time he manifested little or none of the formal self-consciousness, the sheer delight in playing with themes, characters, masks, illusions, structural patterns, the play within a play – the stock-in-trade material of the French playwright from the Renaissance onwards, and which plays a prominent part in the work of most of Camus's contemporaries, Giraudoux, Anouilh, Cocteau, Sartre, right up to Genet and Ionesco. The thematic and structural quotations from Molière, from the Corneille of *L'Illusion comique*, from Marivaux, Musset and Pirandello find no place in Camus's theatre: 'le théâtre n'est pas un jeu.' And it is significant furthermore that, despite his well-known attachment to Greek civilization and his imaginative re-interpretation of the myths of Sisyphus and Prometheus in his philosophical essays, Camus is the only leading dramatist of the 1930s and 1940s apart from Salacrou who did not borrow directly from the Greeks for his own dramatic material.[1]

Not only was Camus in the wrong family for an early initiation into the theatre; he was in the wrong place as well. He was asked in an interview in 1958 what had been his first contact with the theatre but could not remember: 'certainement pas un spectacle: il n'y en avait pas à Alger; ni une retransmission, je n'avais pas de radio.' He considered Algeria at that time to be 'un Sahara théâtral'. In this respect it was not much different from any other colonies or provinces of metropolitan France.[2] If to this day Paris dominates the French theatre even more than London does British theatre, in the 1930s it did so even more. The creation since the Second World War of regional 'Centres Dramatiques' in places like Toulouse, Strasbourg and Saint-Étienne has done much to alleviate this neglect of the French provinces, but in the inter-war period there was no such national policy of cultural decentralization. By the middle of the 1930s the great movement of reform which had been mooted at the beginning of the century by such diverse figures as Antoine, Lugné-Poe, Rouché and Copeau, and launched by the latter, was only just beginning to bear fruit in the shape of the Giraudoux-Jouvet partnership. The gap between the boulevard and the *avant-garde* was being narrowed. But the influence of the reformers still had to permeate through to the provinces – or colonies – and be absorbed from within.

As far as Algeria is concerned it was undoubtedly Camus who took the lead. Between 1935 and 1939 he was the *animateur* of two successive amateur companies of an *avant-garde* nature which provided for those citizens of Algiers who were sufficiently interested high-standard productions of some of the best plays in the world repertory. Exactly how this started is not as clear as one would like it to be, and Camus's own statements, as so often, serve only to complicate the issue. If we are to believe what he said in the 1958 interview, Jacques Copeau was the inspiration and start of it all: '. . . l'histoire du *Vieux Colombier* et les écrits de Copeau m'ont donné l'envie, puis la passion du théâtre. J'ai mis le Théâtre de l'Équipe, que j'ai fondé à Alger, sous le signe de Copeau et j'ai repris, avec les moyens du bord, une partie de son répertoire.' (*TRN*, p. 1711.) The facts, however, do not bear out this statement entirely. Camus's admiration for Copeau was indeed to endure from the time of l'Équipe throughout his career, but this was not the first company that Camus founded. For a continuous period of more than two years before the founding of l'Équipe Camus ran the Théâtre du Travail, a company with a very different aesthetic and ideology. It is instructive to list the repertories of the two companies, including plays which were also *intended* for production but which were shelved for various reasons. They are, retaining the French titles used:

Le Théâtre du Travail, from early 1936 to Spring 1937:
Le Temps du mépris, Malraux's novel, adapted by Camus.
Les Bas-Fonds, Gorki.
La Femme silencieuse, Jonson.
Prométhée enchaîné, Aeschylus, adapted by Camus.
Don Juan, Pushkin.
Révolte dans les Asturies, by Camus and three student friends (banned by the right-wing municipal authorities of Algiers).

Le Théâtre de l'Équipe, from Autumn 1937 to Spring 1939:
La Célestine, Fernando da Rojas.
Retour de l'Enfant Prodigue, Gide, adapted by Camus.
Le Paquebot Tenacity, Vildrac.
Les Frères Karamazov, Dostoevsky, adapted by Copeau.
Le Baladin du Monde Occidental, Synge.

Projected productions:
La Comédie des Bagnes d'Alger, Cervantes, translated by Jeanne-Paule Sicard.
Othello, Shakespeare, translated by Camus.
Les Esprits, Larivey, adapted by Camus.
Caligula, Camus.

Although at first sight it is not obvious from a comparison of the repertories, there was a clean-cut break between the two companies. The issue was Communism. If we wish to discover one of the principal reasons why Camus virtually disowned his association with the Théâtre du Travail and considered that his career began with the Théâtre de l'Équipe we need look no further than this. The Théâtre du Travail was officially committed to the Communist cause, under the aegis of its parent body, the Maison de la Culture, and formed part of the general pattern of *rapprochement* between intellectuals and the masses. Without impugning the integrity of Camus's motives one may observe that the

Communism of his early twenties coincided with a wave of left-wing intellectualism at this time, under eminent leadership. In perhaps the most virulently personal attack upon Camus yet to have appeared (which is saying a lot), Anne Durand has insinuated that Camus's allegiance to the Algerian Communist Party owed everything to the prestige of the cultural figures currently associated with the Communist movement in France: 'N'étions-nous pas à une époque où l'intellectualisme devenait roi? . . . Après les Zola, les Mirbeau, les Anatole France, les Péguy . . . Benda, Romain Rolland, Malraux, Gide, Aragon . . .'[3] For Durand, not only did Camus join the movement for the wrong reasons, but he didn't even go through the right motions once he was in. Ostensibly unaware of Camus's severe tubercular condition during his student days and throughout the period of the Spanish Civil War, Durand attempts to trace back to Camus's earliest writings (in this case *Révolte dans les Asturies*) that bourgeois fondness for easy solutions with which he was to be taxed after the publication of his controversial political and philosophical essay, *L'Homme révolté*, in 1951: 'Que Camus imprégné de doctrine marxiste (ou libertaire) demandant à choisir l'héroïsme (pas n'importe lequel) ne se soit pas engagé, en '37, dans les brigades internationales, cela prouve qu'il préférait la plume au fusil, l'antifascisme héroïquement culturel à l'antifascisme sanguinaire. C'était son affaire.' (p. 64.)

Whatever Camus's motives may have been for joining the C.P., there is little doubt about the authenticity of his reasons for leaving, although controversy exists as to when exactly this happened. He stated in 1955 to his friend, the critic Roger Quilliot, that he left the C.P. in 1935 as a result of Laval's visit to Moscow (amongst other things in order to buy off the Soviet pro-Arab, anti-colonial campaign in so far as it affected the French). Others claim that Camus carried a card until 1937, when he was expelled from the C.P. because of his support for Messali Hadj, leader of the Parti du Peuple Algérien, who accused the Communists of actually conniving at the French Government's suppression of the Arab cause. Even if Camus did not part company with the C.P.

until 1937, an entry in the *Carnets* for March 1936 shows his willingness to be disabused some time before the Messali Hadj crisis.[4] Whichever of these two examples of the Communists' disingenuous North African policy induced Camus to make the break, the vital *personal* influence on Camus over this decision was that of his friend and tutor at the University of Algiers, the philosophy lecturer Jean Grenier. Camus gave the impression after the war that this whole episode was a mistake which he would prefer to forget, just like that other form of total commitment, his first marriage in 1934–5, which was just as ephemeral.

On the artistic plane, however, the results of Camus's Communist allegiance around 1935 are more lasting. Two of the productions of the Théâtre du Travail are of particular interest here (taking 'productions' in a very broad sense to include *Révolte dans les Asturies*). The left-wing commitment of the company is implicit in its manifesto:

> Un Théâtre du Travail s'organise à Alger grâce à un effort collectif et désintéressé. Ce théâtre a conscience de la valeur artistique propre à toute littérature de masse, veut démontrer que l'art peut gagner quelquefois à sortir de sa tour d'ivoire et croit que le sens de la beauté est inséparable d'un certain sens de l'humanité. Ces idées ne sont guère originales. Et le Théâtre du Travail en est bien persuadé. Mais l'originalité ne le préoccupe point. Son effort est de restituer quelques valeurs humaines et non d'apporter de nouveaux thèmes de pensée.
>
> Il fallait adapter les moyens de réalisation aux buts théoriques. De là quelques innovations dans la mise en scène et le décor, grâce à l'application de conceptions nouvelles encore à Alger. (*TRN*, p. 1688.)

The authors were modest in stating that their innovations were unknown in Algiers: they could rightly have claimed that they were fairly new to the whole of the French theatre world. They were in fact borrowed from the German theatre, from Reinhardt, Brecht and Piscator, particularly the latter.

The most curious part of the manifesto is that in which the organizers abjure 'le poncif, la propagande' in the same sentence in which they announce their first production, Camus's own adaptation of Malraux's candidly anti-Nazi novel, *Le Temps du mépris*. The play is unfortunately not extant. It seems clear, however, from a description of the performance by Charles Poncet, that the adaptation was faithful to the spirit of the novel:

> L'ennemi à la croix gammée que combattait farouchement Kassner, c'était aussi celui de chaque spectateur. Cette confrontation héroïque au mal absolu, d'un homme seul, puisant sa force dans la solidarité humaine et le sentiment de la fraternité . . . passait comme un souffle épique sur cette foule tendue qui voyait sur la scène se dérouler son propre combat contre l'esprit dégradant du fascisme. Et quand, au meeting antifasciste de Prague, où Kassner, enfin libéré, recherche Anna et son enfant, un orateur s'adresse à la foule, fiction et tribun tout à la fois, s'éleva l'hymne de la révolte et de l'espoir qui apportait à des millions d'hommes et de femmes une réponse presque charnelle. (*TRN*, p. 1688.)

Clearly, if Poncet's testimony is to be believed, the play was to a large extent a propaganda piece, the climax of which, the anti-Fascist harangue, appealed greatly to the sentiments of the mass audience (Poncet put it at 2,000). This section of the novel, with its speeches from the platform, instructions from the leaders about propaganda, and testimonials from the members of the crowd, lends itself perfectly to the sort of production which Piscator had made fashionable in Germany since the 1920s.

Apart from the obvious theatricality of this section there is little else in Malraux's novel that would make a play of any substance without considerable interpolation by Camus. What happens is very simple. Kassner, a member of the German Communist Party, is interrogated and imprisoned by Nazis, released owing to the self-sacrifice (by impersonation) of an unknown 'comrade', and finally enabled to escape to Prague via the Party's clandestine air network. Here Kassner is reunited with his wife and child in a brief final scene, having sought her without success at the mass meeting. There are few characters other than Kassner; they never meet, and there is little dialogue. The Nazis, the pilot who flies Kassner to safety, and finally Kassner's wife divide the novel into three more or less separate parts. They are given scant individual treatment by the author. In his introduction Malraux concedes the lack of traditional features of the novel, such as the coexistence and confrontation of a *number* of characters, and thus at the same time points to the very obstacles the work would present to adaptation for the stage. The world of his novel 'se réduit à deux personnages, le héros et son sens de la vie; les antagonismes individuels, qui permettent au roman sa complexité, n'y figurent pas. Si j'avais dû donner à des nazis l'importance que je donne à Kassner, je l'aurais fait évidemment en fonction de leur passion réelle, le nationalisme.'[5] The novel contains barely the bones of a scenario for a play: there is only one character about whom much is known, little confrontation with other characters, and few scenes of any dramatic potential – a total contrast with the adapted novels which twenty years later were to earn Camus possibly his greatest successes in the theatre, Dostoevsky's *The Devils* and Faulkner's *Requiem for a Nun*. The novel being as episodic, disjointed and interior as it is, the adaptation must have demanded a considerable amount of skill and ingenuity on Camus's part, and the failure of any script of the play to survive is very much to be regretted.

Style of production has been the salvation of many an episodic script, and it is possible that *Le Temps du mépris* is a case in point. Attention has been drawn to the one really theatrical scene in the novel, which lent itself to the techniques of Reinhardt and Piscator. According to Poncet, the whole play was given the 'agitation' treatment of Piscator in particular: 'le roman de Malraux avait été découpé en de nombreux tableaux qu'animait une mise en scène aux mouvements rapides, utilisant sur les côtés et au fond de la salle, à l'exemple de Piscator, des emplacements inattendus qu'un éclairage fugitif révélait brusquement . . .'

This was clearly the sort of production envisaged for the second play in the repertory of the Théâtre du Travail which was written from an extreme left-wing position, *Révolte dans les Asturies*. This play has suffered the reverse fate of that of *Le Temps du mépris*, having been textually preserved but never performed – it was proscribed by the right-wing municipal authorities of Algiers, it is thought for fear of incurring the diplomatic displeasure of Spain. The play emerged from obscurity only in 1962, on being included by Quilliot in the Pléiade edition of Camus's works; before that date it existed only in the very limited Charlot edition, and was thus unknown to the majority of critics. Even now not much attention is attached to the play since it is known to have been written by Camus in collaboration with three university friends, Bourgeois, Poignant and Jeanne-Paule Sicard. In my view this neglect is undeserved. Admittedly it is difficult to establish just how much was contributed by each collaborator. According to Quilliot, Camus was certain of having written only 'les chœurs', but other sources of information exist: 'D'après Jeanne-Paule Sicard, les textes de radio sont de Poignant; l'interrogatoire (acte 4) de Bourgeois, la scène du Conseil des Ministres d'elle-même et presque tout le reste de Camus, notamment les scènes 2 et 3 de l'acte 2; 1, 2 et 3 de l'acte 2; les pages de présentation et de mise en scène.' (*TRN*, p. 1845.) Quilliot himself considers Scene 3 of Act 2 and the end of Act 4 to be by Camus, and Carl Viggiani detects his influence in the first and last acts, the 'neat structuring', the songs, stage-directions and foreword. But rather than attempt to ascribe responsibility for each part to the individuals, it is more fruitful to understand the atmosphere in which the group worked. Jeanne-Paule Sicard confirms what one suspects on reading the play by stating that Camus dominated the group and that 'la participation des trois co-auteurs n'a existé que dans son sillage'. Making allowances for Camus's immaturity, the play contains the essence of so many of his later themes that it could easily be thought to be entirely by him if one did not know of his collaborators. That small part of the play which is known to have been written by the others accords so well with the rest of the work and with much else that Camus was to write that we may with a reasonable degree of confidence regard *Révolte dans les Asturies* as largely Camus's own creation.

Although it is normally accorded minor status, I believe a fairly full account of the play is justified, in order to give the feel of its dramatic style and themes, and to assess its significance for an understanding of Camus's early political philosophy. The plot has an authentic historical basis. It is a dramatization of the miners' revolt in Asturias in 1934, just before the outbreak of the Spanish Civil War. The issue is presented as a simple clash between right and left, and the authors leave no one in doubt about their allegiance. In the first two acts the miners rebel against the newly elected Lerroux Government, which is supported by the army, police, clergy, and middle and upper classes. The miners proclaim a socialist state, begin to settle their account with the bourgeoisie, and prepare for the onslaught from the Government forces. They are joined by a young Oviedo barber, Pèpe. In the third act the loud-speaker announcements from 'Radio Barcelone' rise to an almost hysterical pitch as the Government regains control. Surrounded by powerful forces, the rebels die heroically at the barricades. In the last act the army disposes of prisoners, and the forces of order and the bourgeoisie congratulate themselves. The disembodied voices of the rebel leaders, including Pèpe, rise up in elegiac lament from different corners of the theatre, expressing the pathos and futility of their action: 'Bientôt les neiges' – 'Et qui se souviendra?'

In both form and content the play derives much from the German theatre of the inter-war years, as revitalized by Reinhardt, Piscator and Brecht, particularly the last two with their respective concepts of 'proletarian' and 'epic' theatre. By 1935 this triumvirate had led the German theatre away from the artistic anarchy and philosophical nihilism which characterized much of Expressionism towards a synthesis which resulted in Brecht's masterpieces of the late 1930s and the 1940s. *Révolte dans les Asturies*, like *Le Temps du mépris*, appears to have been written specifically for the sort of production which Piscator made famous at the Volksbühne and the Theater Piscator. The (for France at this time) bold theatrical conception of *Révolte dans les Asturies* is made evident in the opening stage directions and descriptions of the set – if 'set' is the right word. The authors are at pains to destroy the traditional 'peepshow' effect of the box set:

> Le décor entoure et presse le spectateur, le contraint d'entrer dans une action que des préjugés classiques lui feraient voir de l'extérieur. Il n'est pas devant la capitale des Asturies mais dans Oviedo, et tout tourne autour de lui qui demeure le centre de la tragédie. Le décor est conçu pour l'empêcher de se défendre. De chaque côté des spectateurs, deux longues rues d'Oviedo: devant eux une place publique sur laquelle donne une taverne vue en coupe. Au milieu de la salle, la table du Conseil des Ministres surmontée d'un gigantesque haut-parleur figurant Radio-Barcelone. Et l'action se déroule sur ces divers plans autour du spectateur contraint de voir et de participer suivant sa géométrie personnelle. Dans l'idéal le fauteuil 156 voit les choses autrement que le fauteuil 157. (*TRN*, p. 401.)

If the authors were influenced by Brecht it was by the ideological Brecht, the epic satirist of the bourgeoisie, not the theorist of 'alienation'. Far from contriving a *Verfremdungseffekt* Camus and his friends assimilate the audience as much as possible ('contraint de voir et de participer'). The standard techniques popularized by Piscator are adopted here. One which was of great appeal in the 1930s – audience participation, simulated or otherwise – is used in the first few seconds of the play when the Spanish theme song is acclaimed by two 'planted' actors:

UN AUDITEUR (*dans la salle*). Bravo, bravo!

> *Tandis que le thème est repris par un accordéon, la lumière éclate: au bout d'une rue, un gars appuyé à une arcade, lance de nouveau sa voix:*

Y al son de la pandereta
unos bailes echaremos.

UN AUTRE HOMME (*parmi le public*). S'il est pas bon, le petit!

No more 'plants' are in fact used during the play, and the authors' use of this fashionable device is limited to this one attempt to establish a *rapport* between audience and actors. In another post-Expressionist device, however, Camus and his friends show much more confidence. This is the provision in the script for the full use of all the corners and aisles of the auditorium for the action of the play. Here, among other things, songs are sung, 'des combattants courent autour du public', and 'l'animation traditionnelle de la rue espagnole (reprend)'. Thus the proscenium arch, and the rigid separation of stage and auditorium, are abolished. The audience is assailed on all sides: by actors, by sudden spotlights, by blaring propaganda and statistics from Radio Barcelona. The latter is a device very typical of Piscator's style. In his production of Toller's *Hoppla! Wir Leben!*, for example, statistics concerning the Russian Revolution were flashed on a screen at regular intervals and related to the immediate action – one of the best instances of his belief that: 'The drama is only important in the degree to which it relies on the testimony of document.'[6] In short, the authors of *Révolte dans les Asturies* intended to make full use of the techniques in vogue during the post-Expressionist period: a montage would be built up, juxtaposing light and darkness, music and gunfire, laughter and cries of pain. As Joan Littlewood and Roger Planchon continue to demonstrate some thirty years later, the style is an ideal one for propaganda. The theorists of the German *avant-garde* were the outspoken champions of the proletariat, massed to combat capitalism and eventually – so it was thought – Nazism. For Piscator 'the destiny of the masses is the heroic factor in the new drama'; the middle and upper classes were the targets of the epic dramatist, whose task it was to 'take reality as a point of departure and introduce the elements of accusation, revolution and the new order'.[7]

The medium of accusation was of course satire of a more or less broad nature. In *Révolte dans les Asturies* 'le pharmacien' and 'l'épicier' – *petit bourgeois* tradesmen who have traditionally been the butt of both left- and right-wing French satirists – are thus crudely representative of the conservative and reactionary elements of Spanish society. They bitterly resent the Republic and the possible acquisition of social and economic justice by the peasantry and proletariat: 'tous ces salauds-là, on leur donne un doigt et ils vous bouffent la tête.' For them Lerroux represented a hope of reaction, particularly if, as indeed it turned out, he made allowance in the composition of his cabinet for the aspirations of the Jesuit party, the *Ceda* (Confederación Española de Derechos Autonomos), led by Gil Roblès: 'Toute cette racaille sera bientôt balayée. L'ordre . . . enfin l'ordre . . . enfin la discipline.' The political details and election statistics put over by Radio Barcelone are remarkably accurate. However, the satire is on the whole general, and frequently unsubtle, rather than specifically pertinent to the Spain of 1934:

LE PHARMACIEN. C'est comme ces femmes qu'on fait voter. Leur place est à la maison à raccommoder les chaussettes de leur mari. Ah! le monde a bien changé.

L'ÉPICIER. Moi, jusqu'à l'âge de 25 ans, quand j'allais voter, mon père m'accompagnait et m'indiquait le bon candidat (*portant le verre à ses lèvres*) et comme ça, au moins, il y avaient des traditions qui ne se perdaient pas.

PÈPE (*lui poussant la tête dans son verre*). Et c'est comme ça que tu es aussi con. (*TRN*, p. 407.)

The chemist and the grocer are faint shadows of nineteenth-century French predecessors such as Homais and Prudhomme in their mentality, and as theatrical creations would have been well within the scope of Alfred Jarry's co-rebels at the Lycée de Rennes. The fault, if fault it is, reflects not on the authors of the play so much as on the genre. Oviedo is a microcosm of contemporary Spain, and for that matter of all capitalist countries west of the Soviet Union as far as Camus and his friends were concerned. It was necessary to generalize rather than particularize in order to fill in the background to the insurrection in a series of short, swift-moving scenes which would leave the purpose of the play in no doubt. There was no time or in fact need for subtlety here. Characterization in epic theatre is almost by definition broad, lacking in finesse, larger than life, sometimes literally so, as in Brecht's *Mann ist Mann*, where the brutish British soldiery was played by actors on stilts.

The military fraternity was one of the most consistent targets of this kind of theatre, and was a very legitimate one in this particular play when one bears in mind the part played by the Spanish army in suppressing the miners' revolt. A controversial feature of the suppression was the unprecedented employment in metropolitan Spain of the Foreign Legion and notoriously brutal troops from Morocco, the authorization for which was one of the first ways in which General Franco distinguished himself. Making skilful parodic use of the euphemisms of official communication via Radio Barcelone, Camus and his friends launch a salvo at the Legion:

> Les légionnaires acceptent avec enthousiasme la mission qui leur est confiée; remplacer leurs frères de l'armée espagnole régulière dans une besogne où ils se sont montrés au Maroc d'éminents spécialistes.

Radio Barcelone in fact plays an important satirical role, which is fulfilled either by antiphrastic propaganda:

> Grâce au gouvernement espagnol, héroïquement assisté de l'armée et de la force publique, on vient de sauver en occident les principes essentiels de la démocratie et de la civilisation latine. Mais la répression se passa au milieu de l'humanité et de la générosité qu'il faut faire ressortir pour que le monde sache que le gouvernement espagnol, républicain et constitutionnel, démocratique et parlementaire, en pleine lumière de la critique

universelle, achève de donner, en réprimant une révolution armée puissamment, un exemple jamais égalé de tolérance, d'humanité et de généreuse application des lois. (*TRN*, p. 433.)

or by announcements which are totally at variance with the truth which is being enacted simultaneously on stage:

. . . Il ressort que malgré la gravité des événements, le gouvernement examine la situation avec tout le calme et la sérénité nécessaires.

> *Lumière verte sur la petite scène centrale. Une table recouverte du tapis vert symbolique. Assis autour, six ministres discutent, Lerroux au centre. Alternative d'excitation et d'accablement, gestes mécaniques, un peu ridicules, lents. Un ministre debout s'efforce de convaincre ses collègues, un autre hausse les épaules, un troisième fume, un quatrième se lève et interrompt violemment celui qui parlait. Mouvement général.*

A l'unanimité, le gouvernement a approuvé . . . (*TRN*, pp. 423–4.)

The established institutions of Spain are thus depicted as corrupt and mendacious. The presentation of the rebels and left wing is equally simplistic. They are inspired by fairly commonplace socialist ideals:

SANTIAGO. . . . Il faut des écoles, beaucoup d'écoles. Moi, vous voyez, je ne sais pas lire. C'est mon gars qui me disait les nouvelles, mais il a été tué dans un éboulement. Alors je crois qu'il faudrait en créer des écoles, pour tout le monde. (*TRN*, p. 414.)

The basis of their economic theory, such as it is presented in the play, is nothing more complicated than a plan to abolish money: 'Pour les Bons de travail à la place de l'argent, on est déjà d'accord et ça va fonctionner. . . .' More than this we are not told, nor is it really clear why the miners have rebelled. This half of the dialectic struggle is just as vaguely delineated as the bourgeois half. As the latter stood for greed and hypocrisy, so the rebels stand for moral integrity. They attempt to maintain standards. Looting is forbidden because 'il ne faut pas qu'ils nous la salissent, notre révolution'. Their heroism is exemplary: Ruiz and Leon accept their designation for the suicidal attack on the barracks with stoic pride: 'les deux sortent du rang, saluent du poing et s'en vont sans phrases. Silence des mineurs.' As one would expect in an epic treatment of the masses, the rebels are scarcely individualized. They vary only in the degree to which they love humanity, justice and the physical world, and in their ability to evoke the latter in poetic terms:

> PREMIÈRE VOIX (Santiago). . . . J'ai jamais fait de mal à personne et je me serais bien contenté, mais j'ai pensé aux jeunes. Je crois que je me suis bien battu. Peut-être parce que j'avais plus grand chose à gagner. Aux prochaines neiges, personne ne parlera plus de moi sur la terre.
>
> DEUXIÈME VOIX (Sanchez). . . . J'y ai cru à ma révolution, j'y ai cru. J'ai essayé de lire. Parce que comme ils disent, l'instruction . . . Mais je comprenais mieux avec ma pioche en tapant dans le minérai et quand les étincelles . . .
>
> TROISIÈME VOIX (Antonio). . . . Oui, avant, dans la neige, j'avais pas besoin de penser. Elle est si belle, et puis bien simple. Et quand je suis descendu, j'ai vu les figures noires et l'injustice. Alors, j'ai pensé à ma neige et à ce cri qu'elle jette quand on l'enfonce sous le pied.

The fourth voice is that of the character who most embodies Camus's influence on the play:

> Je suis Pèpe, et Pilar me disait souvent: 'Les plus malheureux, c'est pas ceux qui s'en vont, mais ceux qui restent.' Peut-être que j'aurais aimé rester. Parce qu'il y a le soleil et les fleurs du jardin sur la place, et puis aussi Pilar – mais d'elle je ne peux

rien dire. J'aimais les bals du quartier et on me disait: Pèpe, tu n'es pas sérieux . . . (*TRN*, pp. 436–7.)

But it is not merely in this amorousness and love of the sun and flowers that one detects the prototype of the essential Camusian hero. He is, as Carl Viggiani has briefly observed: 'a very rough draft of the "man in revolt" whose image Camus will not fashion completely until 1951.'[8] Since *Révolte dans les Asturies* has commonly been assumed to be a theatre museum piece of little philosophical significance, this remark deserves further investigation.

At first sight Pèpe, with his earthy vulgarity, would appear to have nothing in common with the tenuous abstract figure who is to be evoked in Camus's major essay. He conceives a sudden intense loathing for the 'épicier' and abuses him with a naturalistic coarseness to be found nowhere else in Camus's theatre. He calls the man 'con', 'gros', 'bête', 'fumier', 'ordure'. Why he should pick on the 'épicier' rather than the 'pharmacien' is not clear. Seconds later, during the pandemonium which results from this harangue, the miners march into the scene and Pèpe breaks free from those who are trying to restrain him: 'Non! . . . Il y a trop longtemps que ça dure. Il fallait que ça crève. Laisse-moi les rejoindre.' He immediately associates himself with the insurrectionary miners, but the exact meaning of 'Il y a trop longtemps que ça dure. Il fallait que ça crève' is not clear in the context of the play. Pèpe has experienced a sudden emotional nausea because of the stupidity and smugness of a particular individual. The fact that the individual is a tradesman and, in terms of the European politics of 1935, a bourgeois reactionary might almost be coincidental – Pèpe himself is nothing more revolutionary than a barber. The grocer has not tyrannized Pèpe personally; he is simply a representative of the section of society which stands to gain most from Lerroux's Government. Examined in the overall context of Camus's work, however, Pèpe's remarks cease to be enigmatic, and the philosophical significance of *Révolte dans les Asturies*, as evidence of the lifelong consistency of Camus's attitude to rebellion and revolution, begins to emerge. Pèpe's protest is a striking anticipation of the language of *L'Homme révolté* fifteen years later: 'Qu'est-ce qu'un homme révolté? Un homme qui dit non . . . Il (ce non) signifie, par exemple: *"Les choses ont trop duré"* . . .' (my italics). The act of rebellion, for Camus, is an assertion of ideals as much as it is a rejection of physical tyranny: 'On notera d'abord que le mouvement de révolte n'est pas, dans son essence, un mouvement égoïste. Il peut avoir sans doute des déterminations égoïstes. Mais on se révoltera *aussi bien contre le mensonge que contre l'oppression.*' (*Essais*, p. 426.) Pèpe is scandalized by the grocer because of his hypocrisy and cynical contempt for democratic standards. Ultimately the man would sanction oppression but it is initially against his mendacity that Pèpe rebels.

Furthermore Pèpe possesses the essential altruism which will characterize the rebel. In the language used by Camus in 1951, rebellion is not necessarily sparked off only in the breast of the oppressed victim; it can be experienced by a neutral onlooker. There results an identification of individuals, with the rebel being a disinterested champion of the victim: 'dans la révolte, l'homme se dépasse en autrui et, de ce point de vue, la solidarité humaine est métaphysique.' In his espousal of the miners' cause and consequent death in its defence Pèpe clearly demonstrates that feeling of solidarity with the mass of humanity which Camus considers to be vital in the rebel. This is why Pèpe is a 'coiffeur', a potential *petit bourgeois* like the grocer and the chemist, and not a miner himself. The point is that he stands to make no material gain out of the insurrection himself, not being a member of the peasantry or industrial proletariat. Pèpe is the prototype of the Camusian rebel, whose self-sacrifice is considered to be all the more authentic for being totally disinterested and altruistic. Pèpe's dramatic 'Non!' does not need to be motivated if one considers him to be a prototype of *L'Homme révolté*. His decision has not been arrived at by a process of logic; on the contrary, it is a sudden surge of keenly felt but ill-defined emotion: 'Si confusément que ce soit, une prise de conscience naît du mouvement de révolte: la perception,

29

soudain éclatante, qu'il y a dans l'homme quelque chose à quoi l'homme peut s'identifier, fut-ce pour un temps. Cette identification jusqu'ici n'était pas sentie réellement.' (*Essais*, p. 424.)

The 'mouvement de révolte' is therefore two things at the same time: a rejection of existing values and the discovery of new ones. Rebellion in the accepted political sense of the word is normally associated with the former of these two acts, but the originality of *L'Homme révolté* – and the cause of its unpopularity with the extreme left wing in 1951 – lies in the importance Camus places on the positive aspect of rebellion, as is made clear from the outset: 'Qu'est-ce qu'un homme révolté? Un homme qui dit non. Mais s'il refuse, il ne renonce pas: c'est aussi un homme qui dit oui, dès son premier mouvement' . . . 'L'esclave révolté dit à la fois oui et non.' This clarifies Pèpe's rebellion and explains its timing. The 'bagarre générale' which is provoked when he attacks the grocer coincides with the 'lointaines explosions', the 'bruit du combat' and the arrival of the insurgent miners in Oviedo. Pèpe's otherwise engimatic 'Non! . . . il y a trop longtemps que ça dure. Il fallait que ça crève. Laisse-moi les rejoindre' is thus a dramatization of the moment of decision – the 'non' coinciding with a 'oui'. The moment is picked out by Camus and isolated scenically in the play: Act I closes with Pèpe half-way between the bourgeoisie and the miners: 'figé entre les deux groupes'. The whole incident, presented in this way, is therefore an anticipation and symbolic materialization of the thesis of *L'Homme révolté*, namely that 'revolt' should be a discovery and preservation of new values as much as, if not more than, the rejection and destruction of the existing (unjust) values. Pèpe is a prototype of Kaliayev and Diego – the rebel who would prefer to love rather than to hate, and who is willing to offer his life as surety for his ideals.

At first sight there would appear to be no counterpart in the play of the false rebel, the nihilist who, like Caligula, Martha, Stepan and Nada in the mature plays, rebels in despair and despair alone, adopting the standards of the enemy, physical or metaphysical, and perpetuating the very injustice which he set out to combat. Mention has been made of the distorted epic division of the characters into noble workers and bourgeois swine. Such a frank political bias imparted to a short play of this nature would appear to preclude the spirit of relativism which is such an important feature of Camus's mature work. And yet closer examination reveals that the miners are not after all seen to adhere to standards of absolute justice. This is made quite clear in Scene 4 of Act 2, where the leader, Sanchez, subjects prisoners to brutal and summary 'justice'. This is a surprising and rapid degradation just a few pages (or minutes in stage time) after Sanchez has warned his friends that: 'Il ne faut pas qu'ils nous la salissent, notre révolution.' Now the grocer is shot on the count of three for being unwilling to turn over his supplies to the rebels, and counter-insurgents are similarly executed after what amounts to a mockery of a trial. Nor are the victims now shown in a bad light. They protest but do not grovel, and put a case which is not altogether unreasonable. The chemist, when summoned to defend the Civil Guard officer, in fact ends his defence with a question which will be the battle-cry of the humanitarian crusader Tarrou: 'Mais cet homme est comme moi. Il ne vous a rien fait à vous. Et puis, c'était son métier, son devoir. Il a peut-être des enfants. De quel droit tuez-vous? De quel droit enfin . . .' (*TRN*, p. 420.)

Sanchez cannot answer the question and condemns the man without qualms. Into the mouth of the next victim the authors put a speech which clearly suggests that they are not unaware of the effect of this scene on the thesis of the play: 'Je n'ai pas besoin d'avocat. Je sais me défendre. *Surtout devant une justice comme ça. Je te méprise.* C'est vrai, j'ai tiré dans le tas. Je n'en ai tué que trois. Tuez-moi, tu verras, il y a encore des bourgeois qui savent mourir.' (*TRN*, p. 421, my italics.)

The standards of the rebels are thus, on closer examination, by no means beyond reproach. Indeed at this early stage of the insurrection the rebels have descended lower than the enemy they are fighting. This is once more an anticipation of an important theme of *L'Homme révolté*: 'Il s'agit de savoir si l'innocence, à partir du moment où elle agit, ne peut s'empêcher de tuer.' In his lament from the grave at the end of the play Sanchez voices optimism about his methods: 'Tant de morts, tant de morts. Mais quelque chose viendra. Et moi, je leur dirai: "La révolution, ça se fait pas avec un éventail."' Sanchez does not regret the necessity of breaking bourgeois eggs to make a revolutionary omelette. Despite his very short scenes and few lines he stands out never-theless as a rough draft of Stepan Fedorov in *Les Justes*, who is quite prepared to perpetuate murder and terror for the sake of a hypothetical future Utopia. The point must not be laboured of course. Condemnation of him is only fleetingly implicit; no-where is there the thematic stress on *limits* which is an important feature, if not the whole message, of Camus's mature plays. The fact nevertheless remains that Sanchez basically incarnates im-moderate rebellion (or 'revolution', to use the term we established in Chapter 1) of the sort which is to be the target of *L'Homme révolté*. In him and Pèpe we may thus detect the seeds of the author's mature thought as early as his twenty-third year, some three years before they begin to germinate fully in *Caligula*.

As well as adumbrating the crucial revolt/revolution conflict, *Révolte dans les Asturies* announces the dawning of the 'absurd' in Camus's sensibility, although the two concepts are as yet only loosely linked. One paragraph of the short preface to the play unmistakably anticipates *Le Mythe de Sisyphe*, although in a manner which is nothing less than hermetic at this stage of Camus's development: 'Il suffit que cette action conduise à la mort, comme c'est le cas ici, pour qu'elle touche à une certaine forme de grandeur qui est particulière aux hommes: l'absurdité.' (*TRN*, p. 399.) Within the play itself the absurd is dealt with even less explicitly than revolt, which is not surprising, since the play is principally a propaganda work about a precise social and political issue. A metaphysical overtone does not become apparent until the last scene of the play, when the voices of the eight dead rebels stress the fragility and impermanence of their existence and the futility of their sacrifice:

CINQUIÈME VOIX. On nous a tirés au sort.
SIXIÈME VOIX. C'était pour le camion.

(The manner in which these two particular rebels, Ruiz and Leon, were selected for death – by drawing lots – can be regarded as an instance of Camus's tendency to provide the example before the formulation. The random selection of victims by the absurd is here presented in a material form; only later, in *Caligula* and *Le Mythe de Sisyphe*, will it be conceptualized.)

QUATRIÈME VOIX. Bientôt les neiges.
TROISIÈME VOIX. Et qui se souviendra?
SEPTIÈME VOIX. Et les flûtes de chez nous . . . C'est pas possible que ça soit pour rien.
HUITIÈME VOIX. Si Dieu veut.
DEUXIÈME VOIX. Bientôt les neiges.
PREMIÈRE VOIX. Et qui se souviendra?

The scene is intended to be played in darkness. The rebels are thus invisible, nameless, disembodied. The play has thus come full circle from the last line of the preface, as it were: 'L'Histoire n'a pas gardé leurs noms', and ends by stressing the absurdity of death.

I have given this long account of *Révolte dans les Asturies* because I believe its importance has been underestimated as a seminal work in the evolution of the rebel. As a piece of theatre, however, its merit should not be exaggerated. It makes interesting reading from the historical angle; it combines a genuinely touching pathos with lyricism in the choruses; and Radio Barcelone is handled with an irony which is amusing to all who have had any experience of the press and radio of the Latin world. Yet, as the text now stands, it is doubtful if it could serve as anything other than 'travaux pratiques' for a group of Roger Planchon's trainee actors. Even making generous allowance for the improvised epic sequences – street scenes, fights, deployment of the opposing forces – the play is short, running for perhaps fifty minutes. This is not too short for one of the *Lehrstücke*, in which Brecht poses a problem and goes briskly about his business, manipulating plot and ideological dialectic. But then Brecht had the secret of the

33

ideal balance between theatre and drama. *Révolte dans les Asturies*, however, is a potentially *theatrical* play (despite the excessive length of some of the radio documentary passages), but contains little genuine *dramatic* substance. The moral and psychological issues – Pèpe's decision to join the rebellion, the brutality forced upon the rebels by the pressure of events – pass in a few seconds without any dramatic exploitation of the conflict between alternatives, and are only fully understood in the context of Camus's subsequent work, particularly *L'Homme révolté*.

Révolte dans les Asturies is thus a rather insubstantial semi-lyrical, semi-epic *tableau*, an interesting attempt to adapt northern European theatre techniques to the Mediterranean world. The theatre of 'agitation' was later admitted by Camus to be a false start, an artistic impasse as far as his own career was concerned, and, with the exception of one semi-aberration, *L'État de siège*, was behind Camus after 1937. His irrepressible individualism was in fact quietly simmering at the very time the Théâtre du Travail was in full swing. In January 1937 he made his first note in the *Carnets* for *Caligula*, the hero of which, solipsism incarnate, could not be further removed from the theoretical paragon of Communism and Communist theatre.

3 *Caligula*

La mort est là, comme l'irréfutable preuve de l'absurdité de la vie.

Malraux, *La Voie royale*

Jean Grenier – quel merveilleux ami, toujours vous ramenant vers l'essentiel malgré vous! Grenier fut mon premier maître et il l'est resté.

Camus

Caligula is Camus's first completely original play and undoubtedly his best and most enduring. Although it was not performed until 1945, *Caligula* was drafted in a fairly complete form by 1939 and was intended to be put on by the Théâtre de l'Équipe. Camus himself, since he played the lead in most of the productions of his two companies, would have taken the part of Caligula. As he was to put it later with characteristic irony: 'Les acteurs débutants ont de ces ingénuités. Et puis j'avais 25 ans, âge où l'on doute de tout, sauf de soi. La guerre m'a forcé à la modestie . . .' (*TRN*, p. 1727.)

The play made an immediate impact when it was first performed in 1945. It opened on 26 September at the Théâtre Hébertot, ran for nearly a year, and was revived professionally at least three times during Camus's lifetime, in 1950, 1957 and 1958. It seems clear that the initial success was due at least in part to the 'creation' of the role of Caligula by the brilliant but at that time unknown Gérard Philipe, under the direction of Paul Oettly – no small stroke of luck for Camus. Yet at the same time the play possessed an intrinsic appeal for the spectators of 1945. It dealt with a theme which appeared clear-cut and relevant in its political implications (if at times difficult and obscure in its metaphysical premisses): the dangers of philosophical absolutism. This theme is put across in a play with a simple and linear plot which nevertheless holds a very great theatrical appeal. It combines on the one hand, particularly in those scenes in which Caligula is alone with

35

just one of the four other leading characters, moments of very effective and legitimate pathos, and on the other hand the most powerful verbal and scenic rhetoric of the sort that is virtually inescapable in any play about Gaius Caligula. Finally for the audiences of 1945 there was the ghoulish and macabre fascination of the hero himself at a time when Europe and particularly France were emerging from the chaos created by Hitler and Mussolini, two imperial megalomaniacs whose personalities bore many superficial likenesses to that of Caligula. The legitimacy or otherwise of this interpretation is an important point in any discussion of *Caligula*, and will be examined in due course.

The play is based on the last three years in the life of Gaius Caesar – nicknamed 'Caligula' in his childhood because he wore the military boot *caliga* – who was one of the maddest of the Julio-Claudian Emperors described by Suetonius in his *Lives of the Caesars*. Suetonius' sensational biography, more of a collection of lurid atrocities and murders allegedly committed by Caligula than a biography in a modern sense, is ideally suited to Camus's purpose as suggested by one of his first notes for the play in January 1937: 'Caligula ou le sens de la mort'. In so far as the facts set out by Suetonius are 'facts' at all, Camus sticks fairly closely to the historical outlines of Caligula's life and death. Gaius Caesar 'Caligula' was born on 31 August A.D. 12 and stabbed to death in January A.D. 41, the victim of a conspiracy led by two colonels of the guard, Cassius Chaerea and Sabinus. At his death Caligula had been emperor for nearly four years, a period which became increasingly a reign of terror. Suetonius' account is a colourful fabric of anecdotes about the social and political scandals, surrealistic obscenities, rape, murder, incest and miscellaneous lunacies attributed to Caligula, and which culminated in his inevitable assassination. Camus has incorporated many of these features of Caligula's madness in his play: his moon fixation and his fondness for staring at himself in a mirror, for example, are two of the idiosyncrasies which are potentially most suggestive, from a symbolic point of view, in a play about metaphysical *speculation* and illusion and reality. Other legendary deeds or

customs of Caligula are built into the plot without any significant
modification and serve to motivate the assassination on which the
play ends. Caligula reputedly abused women in front of their
husbands, forced the rich to bequeath their wealth to the state,
tortured a child to death in its father's sight, and obliged poets to
lick their slates clean at a competition. Many similar incidents are
laid at his door. And yet although Camus kept to the broad outlines of Caligula's career and relied entirely on the incidents
described in Suetonius for the plot of the play, he nevertheless
stated that in its fundamentals *Caligula* is not a historical play. An
examination of its plot, characterization and philosophical theme
soon makes it clear why this claim is justified.

Camus opens his play at the heart of a crisis and on the brink of
disaster. The whole of the first act takes place at a time when
Caligula has been Emperor for about a year. By all accounts he has
been a very good one: 'tout allait trop bien. Cet empereur était
parfait.' However, his sister and mistress Drusilla has died, and his
immediate reaction has been to flee from his palace into the
Roman countryside. For the semi-comic chorus of inane patricians
this is the natural effect on 'un sentimental' of the loss of a lover.
Caligula returns after three days, exhausted and dishevelled, and
informs his friend, the freed slave Hélicon, that he has been looking for the moon: 'Mais je ne suis pas fou et même je n'ai jamais
été aussi raisonnable. Simplement je me suis senti tout d'un coup
un besoin d'impossible.' Contrary to the belief of the patricians,
'cette mort n'est rien'. Caligula has been affected not by the
personal loss of Drusilla but by his discovery of the absurd:
'Les hommes meurent et ils ne sont pas heureux.' To attempt to
possess the moon, to hold it in his hands – a symbol of impossible
attainment – is his reaction to the effect which his sudden awareness of the absurd has made on his sensibility. Just as it is impossible for man to evade death so it is impossible for Caligula to
hold the moon between his hands. Camus makes Caligula the
first man in history to rebel against this certainty. He will not
accept the message of the absurd in its most striking manifestation,
that the inevitability of death means that man's happiness on this

earth must be relative, not absolute. Or rather he accepts the message but follows it through with a 'logic' which no man previously has been lucid or powerful enough to pursue.

The men around Caligula are the realists, the relativists, who, like the ordinary human beings who surround Anouilh's rebel heroines, survive more or less happily, usually by means of illusions, sometimes by lies, always by compromise. But Caligula is not one of Anouilh's frail young women. He is the Roman Emperor, and when he cries 'tout, autour de moi, est mensonge, et moi, je veux qu'on vive dans la vérité!' he has the power to make the whole world discover the absurd. The remainder of the play is devoted to this education and its consequences. Still obsessed by the moon, Caligula becomes for the mass of mankind, represented by the patricians, a *lunatic* absolutist. It is in his philosophical interpolation that Camus makes the most ingenious use of his legendary theme. His Caligula turns upon society, to which he is superior by virtue of his intelligence and sensitivity and unique sudden vision of truth. There have been many rebels before in French literature, particularly in the Romantic period: outcasts, hypersensitive misfits, *poètes maudits*, challenging society in all its established might with no certainty of achieving anything other than their own destruction. But Caligula operates initially from strength. Thus much of the power of the climax to Act I stems from a combination of two factors. Camus is using a semi-mythic, semi-historical theme which preconditions an audience in much the same way as do the myths of Troy, Thebes and Argos as used by so many of Camus's contemporaries in the French theatre. We know that Caligula was a tyrant, a monster of depravity, who eventually went too far and was assassinated. It is clear as Act I draws to a close that Caligula is about to become all that Suetonius said he was. And yet Camus, with a fair degree of credibility and ingenuity, has created a highly pregnant first act interval by making it clear that it is the tyrant who has the ideals. For once the outsider who has taken upon himself the task of transforming society is endowed with immense power. With such credibility in fact that at least two critics have persuaded themselves that Suetonius' characteristic line *hactenus quasi de principe, reliqua ut de monstro narranda sunt* means that Caligula was a perfect emperor until the death of Drusilla but thereafter became irrevocably mad and evil;[1] whereas the Caligula portrayed by Suetonius showed signs of depravity during his adolescence, went mad for physiological reasons (and not overnight), possessed little or no virtue, and was not irrevocably unhinged by the death of Drusilla who was only one of three sisters (but admittedly the favourite) with whom Caligula allegedly committed incest. Thus it is not only because he grafted the absurd on to a historical situation that Camus rightly disclaimed any intention of creating a historical play: the very factual basis of the history in the first place is unsound.

The enigmatic reshaping of the legendary material is further complicated in Act 1 by the fact that Camus has taken care to enlist our sympathy for Caligula right from the start. Every character who appears in the play at any time is presented at the earliest possible moment in Act 1, and Caligula comes out of the juxtaposition very well. On the one hand there is the choric group of more or less anonymous patricians. They are fatuous, petty, hypocritical figures, symbolizing the supine conservatism of the establishment and serving the same function as the chemist and the grocer in *Révolte dans les Asturies*. But between them and Caligula is juxtaposed a second group of characters, the four supporting roles, who, in their relationships either with one another or with Caligula, create the philosophical ambiguity – and subtlety – of the play. Each of these characters has some sort of bond with Caligula. With Hélicon it is social. A freed slave who acts as the Emperor's henchman, he is a witty cynic who loathes the establishment as much as Caligula does but for personal reasons. He throws himself enthusiastically into the task of organizing the disruption of society without the philosophical understanding of why, according to Caligula's logic, such action may be considered justified. A somewhat similar figure is Caesonia, 'la vieille maîtresse', who has a purely sensual relationship with Caligula. She fills what will be an increasingly familiar slot in

39

Camus's work, that of a sort of composite wife-mother-mistress figure (her prototype was the mature Pilar in *Révolte dans les Asturies*). With an appropriately dog-like fidelity both Hélicon and Caesonia will stick by Caligula in his last moments. With the far more important characters of Scipion and Cherea, however, we move to much higher levels of human attachment. Scipion, the young poet whose father has been murdered by Caligula, is allied to him by a spiritual and emotional bond: 'quelque chose en moi lui ressemble pourtant. La même flamme nous brûle le cœur.' He is Caligula's only successful pupil, the only one who understands the point of Caligula's brutal pedagogy and who becomes aware of and accepts the absurd in all its implications. Irrevocably contaminated, he refuses to join in the conspiracy and leaves Rome, incapable of action either for or against Caligula. Cherea, the last and most important of these four characters, understands and to a certain extent sympathizes with both Caligula and Scipion. He is an intellectual, a lover of books, a retiring, Apollonian figure contrasting with the Dionysian Caligula. He knows what has happened to Caligula, and what is happening to Scipion, through having himself resisted the philosophical implications of the absurd when younger: 'j'ai fait taire en moi ce qui pouvait lui ressembler.' A moderate and a respecter of peace and compromise, Cherea will assume increasing importance during the course of the play as he is called down from his ivory tower to act in the name of the sanity which is more important to him than idealism. Put simply, in the terms from *Le Mythe de Sisyphe* which I explained in Chapter 1, Cherea, like most people whether they are aware of it or not, believes in a qualitative ethic – 'je crois qu'il y a des actions qui sont plus belles que d'autres', whereas Caligula does not – 'Je crois que toutes sont équivalentes.' As Caligula says to Caesonia at the end of Act 1, 'Tout est sur le même pied: la grandeur de Rome et tes crises d'arthritisme': there is no hierarchy of values. The remaining three acts are devoted to Caligula's systematic destruction of relative values.

Act 2 takes place when Caligula's campaign is three years old. The patricians are outraged by Caligula's atrocities and have met at Cherea's house to plot the Emperor's assassination. Acts 3 and 4, taking place in the days or weeks immediately following, continue the movement towards the inevitable consummation. Much of the material of these three acts consists of the more notorious of Suetonius' incidents dramatized. There is one major set-piece per act: one of Caligula's characteristically nerve-racking banquets in Act 2, his Venus-masquerade in Act 3 and the poetry competition in Act 4. A possible criticism of the play from the structural point of view is that there is too great a lapse of time between Act 1 and the remaining three acts. Thus without making any formal use of flashbacks Camus spends a lot of time, for almost three-quarters of the play, presenting atrocities of the sort which motivated the plotting which began as early as the beginning of Act 2. One feels that a dramatist with a surer grasp of dramatic form would have either situated Act 2 much closer in time to the beginning of Caligula's campaign and kept the start of the resistance movement entirely for Act 3, or else made almost the whole of Act 3 one long flashback. My own feeling, however, is that the leisurely, chronological (and some would say old-fashioned and typically Camusian) movement of these three acts is not a bad thing, considering the complexity of the philosophical arguments which have assailed an audience throughout Act 1. The audience now has time to digest Camus's thesis, especially as it is clarified and developed during the crucial scenes between Caligula, Cherea and Scipion, while at the same time enjoying the black comedy of the patrician scenes. The long confrontation with Cherea in Act 3, Scene 6, and with Scipion at the end of the poetry competition (Act 4) prepare for the anagnorisis, for Caligula's admission to Caesonia: 'soyons justes, je n'ai pas seulement la bêtise contre moi, j'ai aussi la loyauté et le courage de ceux qui veulent être heureux.'

I discussed in Chapter 1 one of the major pitfalls into which interpreters of Camus's theatre commonly fall: the temptation to schematize *grosso modo* into two periods, the 'absurd' period (up to 1945) and the period of 'revolt' thereafter. The two concepts are in fact indissociable throughout Camus's theatre, although of course the emphasis may vary from play to play. *Caligula* illustrates this better than most, partly for the reason that a large number of manuscripts and variants exist, from the first jottings in Camus's *Carnets* in 1937 and continuing through the published editions of the play in 1945, 1947 and 1958. Take first of all the absurd as a theme of the play. Here it is important to realize just what Camus has made of the Caligula-Drusilla incident in Suetonius, and to understand why he has singled it out from amidst a mass of equally grotesque incidents. The responsibility for making Caligula's transformation an abrupt one and attributing it to the death of Drusilla belongs entirely to Camus. What he sought in his raw material was an incident which he could refashion to illustrate the 'meaning of death'; i.e. the mathematical certainty of death makes one aware of 'le caractère dérisoire de cette habitude, l'absence de toute raison profonde de vivre, le caractère insensé de cette agitation quotidienne et l'inutilité de la souffrance' (*Le Mythe de Sisyphe*). Camus also wished to show the *manner* in which this meaning is perceived. Far from emerging as a result of a 'slow incubation' as one critic has suggested, the absurd bursts upon the consciousness as a result of a *sudden* access of lucidity. *Le Mythe* once again makes the point clear: 'Le sentiment de l'absurdité au détour de n'importe quelle rue peut frapper à la face de n'importe quel homme. Tel quel, dans sa lumière sans rayonnement, il est insaisissable. Mais cette difficulté même mérite réflexion.' 'Reflection' – this is exactly the reaction which contact with death provokes in Caligula, according to Scipion: 'Il s'est avancé vers le corps de Drusilla. Il l'a touché avec deux doigts. *Puis il a semblé réfléchir*, tournant sur lui-même, et il est sorti d'un pas égal.' Thus the death of the beloved is the occasion for the 'naissance misérable' and is assimilated to the category of banal discovery from which the absurd draws its 'commencement dérisoire'. Credit must go to Camus for the ingenuity with which he has adapted this incident in a way which is credible in the context of Caligula's life, and at the same time is perfectly consistent with the author's view of death and other manifestations of the absurd in his work at this time.

Le Mythe de Sisyphe serves perfectly adequately to explain the 'absurd' basis of *Caligula*, and Camus's first notes for the play in his *Carnets* make it clear that the whole of the play as it was first conceived would have been explicable in these terms. The scenario which Camus sketched out in January 1937 is built around Caligula and Drusilla and it was not until near the end that he proposed to deal with 'Mort de Drusilla. Fuite de Caligula.' When Camus rejected this project and drafted his first manuscript he still portrayed a hero obsessed with the horror of his discovery, but the emphasis changed slightly. Partly because of the difficulty of communicating the absurd on the stage without a totally different concept of form and style – a problem which the so-called 'absurd playwrights', notably Beckett and Ionesco, attempted to solve in a radical way – but mainly because of his own philosophical development, Camus gave the play a new slant, and one to which *Le Mythe* would not be relevant. For just as Camus stressed that 'Ce qui m'intéresse, je veux encore le répéter, ce ne sont pas tant les découvertes absurdes. Ce sont leurs conséquences', so in *Caligula* he revealed an increasing concern for the moral and philosophical consequences of the Emperor's reaction at the expense of a purely dramatic presentation of the discovery which unleashed it. In other words revolt will have just as important a part to play in *Caligula* as the absurd. But the consequences examined in *Le Mythe* of the discovery that 'aucune morale, ni aucun effort ne sont *a priori* justifiables devant les sanglantes mathématiques qui ordonnent notre condition' are very different from those examined in the more mature versions of *Caligula* from 1938 onwards. The play is still basically the tragedy of the man who is unable to maintain the tension of the two terms of the 'pari déchirant et merveilleux de l'absurde', but his way out of the impasse does not correspond to any of the three possibilities discussed in *Le Mythe*.

In *Le Mythe* Camus rejected the two traditional, but to him unsatisfactory, reactions to the discovery of the absurd, which result from the cancellation of one of the terms. These were (1) physical suicide, i.e. suppressing term A (the self) and maintaining

43

term B (the world – inscrutable, irrational and meaningless), and thus capitulating to the absurd (the unbearable relationship A plus B), and (2) philosophical suicide, the leap of faith, according to which term A, although preserved as a *living* entity, is destroyed as an agent of intellectual inquiry. In other words term A, the self, does not literally commit suicide but simply ceases to think, and in this sense commits *philosophical* suicide. Term B is negated: reasoned scrutiny of the world is rejected and refuge is sought in religion, with the effect of escaping from, rather than capitulating to, the absurd. The third possible reaction, and the one advocated by Camus, requires both terms to be maintained in equilibrium: the absurd is preserved. *Caligula,* much more from the time of its drafting in 1938 than probably at its conception, illustrates a fourth possible reaction, and one not examined in *Le Mythe.* The play is about the danger of disturbing the equilibrium not by the physical or philosophical suicide of A but by an attack upon B. The self both combats the absurd in a sense and also allies with it to universalize an awareness of it in the whole of humanity, which is a component of term B. The result is that the relationship A plus B is broken in a welter of universal homicide and chaos. B is partly destroyed, and A totally, for in the end the self virtually commits suicide: Camus accentuated this point by adding to his 1947 version of the play the scene in Act 3 in which the Old Patrician informs Caligula of the plot, to which news the latter remains indifferent. Caligula is unable to live the difficult compromise, to walk the tightrope between *Tout* (the vision of an ideal world, in which the totality of human experience would be logical and at the same time morally acceptable) and on the other hand *Rien* (the evidence of the real world, where nothing is tolerable: Nihilism). Camus originally used as a working title for the play *Caligula ou le Joueur,* and we may see the Emperor as the man who gambles on the absolute, who tries to pierce the 'walls of the absurd' by being 'logique jusqu'à la fin'. Thus, like *Le Mythe de Sisyphe, Caligula* illustrates a quantitative ethic. The difference is that now it is not an ethic of creation, aiming at a positive although qualified happiness, but on the contrary an ethic of destruction. The difference between the two consequences is the difference between *L'Étranger* and *Caligula*, as Carina Gadourek has observed:

> Au lieu de se faire le professeur de l'humanité qui pousse le reste des mortels dans la voie de la vérité et de la liberté, un tempérament plus calme pouvait décider d'aller son chemin tout seul et sans discours, sans essayer de rien changer pour les autres. Ainsi considéré, Meursault s'oppose à Caligula comme le Rien au Tout.[2]

As well as being of the greatest importance for a study of the absurd, *Caligula* is thus crucial in the development of the theme of revolt. For not only does the play demonstrate the catastrophic consequences of a quantitative ethic allied to a combative attitude towards the absurd – taking the form of absolute revolt – but it goes a considerable part of the way towards establishing a more valid alternative. From the start Camus had stressed the provisional nature of *Le Mythe*. It was a *point de départ* and could hardly be anything else in view of the highly abstract circumstances in which he placed the four manifestations of the absurd hero. But this is where the importance of Cherea comes in. Camus makes it clear that he has a philosophical understanding of the absurd, although he has doubtless not made contact with it by means of such a traumatic experience as Caligula's. He is nevertheless an individual in a much more concrete situation than the four modern descendants of Sisyphus. He lives in a world of contingency, and is lucid enough to determine the conditions and consequences for others of any choice he is forced to make. His articulate objections to Caligula's form of revolt are a clear indication that even before *Le Mythe* was written (September 1940–March 1941) Camus was finding the highly personal ethic expounded in that work to be an untenable solipsism in the face of current political events.

Although in his earliest form prone to flippancy and cynicism –

characteristics which Camus appears to have redistributed to Hélicon whom he created later – Cherea existed in *Caligula* as a fairly well-developed character right from the start. Thus as early as 1938 he understood the nature of Caligula's revolt, his desire for the identification of thought with action, the ideal with the real: 'par Caligula et pour la première fois dans l'histoire, la pensée agit et le rêve rejoint l'action. Il fait ce qu'il rêve de faire.' The peril of absolutism is equally clear to him: 'qu'un seul être soit pur, dans le mal ou dans le bien, et notre monde est en danger,' and in the same harangue to the patricians in Act 2 he envisages the full consequences: 'oui, laissons continuer Caligula. Poussons-le dans cette voie. Organisons cette folie. Un jour viendra où il sera seul devant un empire plein de morts ou de parents de morts.' However, it is particularly in the crucial confrontation with Caligula in Act 3, Scene 6, that Cherea, in his advocacy of moderation and condemnation of extremism, most explicitly anticipates the concept of 'limited revolt' and the *qualitative* ethic which are to be the most salient features of Camus's thinking and writing after the war. Cherea assumes his 'devoirs d'homme' and in acknowledging a moral responsibility towards society, despite being tempted by the same 'logical' conclusion as Caligula, he announces the communal ethic of human solidarity which is to be extolled in *La Peste* and *L'Homme révolté*.

To situate this anti-nihilist and positive aspect of *Caligula* more accurately in the context of Camus's developing thought we may refer to a work which is much more the contemporary of the play than *La Peste* or *L'Homme révolté*. This is the series of four *Lettres à un ami allemand* of 1943–4. In the fourth letter Camus, addressing his fictitious German friend, might almost be paraphrasing Cherea in the scene just described:

> Nous avons longtemps cru ensemble que ce monde n'avait pas de raison supérieure et que nous étions frustrés. Je le crois encore d'une certaine manière. Mais j'en ai tiré d'autres conclusions que celles dont vous me parliez alors et que, depuis tant d'années, vous essayez de faire entrer dans l'Histoire.

And in the same letter, even when the butt of Camus's forensic eloquence is more obviously the brutal realism of Nazi ambition, the analogy with Caligula's pedagogic method is none the less striking:

Vous n'avez jamais cru au sens de ce monde et vous en avez tiré l'idée que tout était équivalent et que le bien et le mal se définissaient selon qu'on le voulait. Vous avez supposé qu'en l'absence de toute morale humaine ou divine les seules valeurs étaient celles qui régissaient le monde animal, c'est-à-dire la violence et la ruse. Vous en avez conclu que l'homme n'était rien et qu'on pouvait tuer son âme, que dans la plus insensée des histoires la tâche d'un individu ne pouvait être que l'aventure de la puissance, et sa morale, le réalisme des conquêtes. Et à la vérité, moi qui croyais penser comme vous, je ne voyais guère d'argument à vous opposer, sinon un goût violent de la justice qui, pour finir, me paraissait aussi peu raisonnée que la plus soudaine des passions.

Où était la différence? C'est que vous acceptiez légèrement de désespérer et que je n'y ai jamais consenti. (*Essais*, p. 240.)

The similarities between Camus's objections to Nazism and Cherea's opposition to Caligula are so great that one can easily understand how the audiences of 1945 believed that the play was intended as a direct comment on the contemporary Fascist cataclysm. Camus however was firmly opposed to this association and argued in a letter to Jean Paulhan: 'although it was conceived and written in 1938, events have given it a meaning which it did not originally have . . . it was as I conceived it a drama of the mind outside all contingencies.'[3] But all that Camus is saying here is that he did not set out to write a consciously committed work containing deliberate allusions to German or Italian Fascism. There is a sense in which Fascism can be philosophical and intellectual as much as political, and a tyrant does not have to be as allusively

47

characterized as Sartre's Aegisthus in *Les Mouches* or Camus's own la Peste in *L'État de siège* to be considered remotely relevant to the political climate of Europe in the 1930s and 1940s. Of course *Caligula* originated as a 'drama of the mind', but in the letters to his imaginary German friend Camus made it clear that as far as he was concerned Nazism stemmed from precisely the same sort of drama of the mind: the sudden perception that there are no absolute standards and no ultimate divine sanction. The way was clear for the 'adventurers' and 'conquerors' of the twentieth century to misinterpret and exploit to their own advantage two of the most pregnant hypotheses of the nineteenth century: 'God is dead' (Nietzsche) and 'If God does not exist, anything is permissible' (Dostoevsky).

In its philosophical atmosphere *Caligula* is very much a characteristic play of its age. Take first of all the subject-matter. There is an undoubted affinity between *Caligula* and the numerous plays on classical Greek themes of the 1930s and 1940s. This rather phenomenal revival has by now been well discussed and documented.[4] Some of the lesser playwrights no doubt hoped to cash in on the lucrative vogue established by Giraudoux and Cocteau (for example André Roussin with his *Hélène ou la Joie de vivre*), and other plays, notably *Les Mouches* and *Antigone*, could only have been performed under the nose of the German censor in their classical guise. But the movement is of greater significance when interpreted out of this strict context of theatrical fad or political contingency, and when seen in the light of Jung and Kérényi's research into archetypes and the collective unconscious. The modern French dramatist, to a far greater extent than his contemporaries in other countries, has made use of a framework of crucial situations and relationships involving death, violence, exile and madness in which to set the crisis of the Western moral consciousness in the modern age, especially during its time of sharpest focus: the Second World War and the events immediately leading up to it. It is not satisfactory to suggest that the modern French return to classical mythology is no more than convenient utilization of existing material, a sort of cultural tomb-robbing as George Steiner sees it, in order to indulge in *jeux d'esprit*. Classical tombs may well have been robbed in France between 1925 and 1950, and the genre has undoubtedly been endowed with an aura of frivolity – some might put it as strongly as sacrilege – by some of the work of Cocteau and Giraudoux. Yet on the whole it was not for easy gain that bodies were lifted from Troy, Thebes and Argos and resurrected in Paris. The very limited range of Greek myths used, and the striking obsession with one or two – rarely the ones which made the great tragedies of the seventeenth century, it should be noted – seem to suggest that the theft was a genuine response to needs of the French collective unconscious, a theft carried out in the dark shadow of a handful of archetypes. Well over a dozen leading French authors each wrote an average of almost two 'neo-Greek' plays during this period. Yet of the enormous range of themes and characters which were fully exploited in the Renaissance, the number transposed to the modern period is small. Oedipus and Jocasta, Antigone and Creon, Orestes and Electra, these are the characters and relationships which dominate the age, reflecting, perhaps, some of the most significant aspects of the French malaise at this time: increasing sensitivity to the arrogance of power, a growing consciousness in intellectuals of metaphysical alienation, and a general re-examination of personal (particularly sexual?) values. Few writers of the late 1930s were more concerned with these and kindred dilemmas than Camus. And yet he is one of the few members of the generation of French dramatists who came to the fore at this time who did not draw directly on Greek mythology. He was in fact opposed to the movement, and spoke of the weariness of the theatregoing public with contemporary versions of the *Atridae*. In particular he associated this kind of play with the ostentatious intellectualism of Giraudoux ('l'un des écrivains les moins faits pour le théâtre'), with his constant recourse to 'la grâce, l'esprit, le conventionnel et le charmant'. But Camus could not resist the pull of the classical archetype at this time, for *Caligula*, although Roman and in its factual essentials historical as opposed to Greek and mythological, acts upon our consciousness in much the same way as do the myths adapted by Gide, Sartre, Anouilh and the others. Suetonius was a scandalmonger and propagandist. A healthy corrective to the *Lives of the Caesars* is Tacitus, but Tacitus' Life of Gaius Caligula is not extant. Thus of the Julio-Claudian Emperors Caligula is the one whose character has been, and always will be, embellished with all the lusts and quirks which are commonly attributed in the popular imagination to the monster-tyrant figures of history. The raw material which Camus has used for the plot and characters of his play is prurient sensationalism and highly suspect history, destined to be for ever doubted but never completely corrected. It is tempting to suggest that it is precisely because it is such material, whether Camus knew it to be such or not, that it has suited his purpose so well. Caligula has attained an almost mythical stature, rivalling in the popular imagination such figures as Herod, Attila the Hun, Genghis Khan, the Borgias, Richard III, Ivan the Terrible – and Adolf Hitler. He is a giant of depravity and tyranny who cannot, for want of a historical corrective, be reduced in size by comparison with the other eminent figures in the field at this time: Nero, Claudius, Tiberius, Galba, Vitellius and Domitian. Of all the *Lives*, that of Caligula, with its atmosphere of terror, suspicion and decadence and its twin themes of death and gratuitousness, is the ideal raw material out of which to forge a myth of the absurd.

No one need be surprised to know that it was Jean Grenier, who played such a crucial role in Camus's political and philosophical evolution at this time, who put Camus on to the Caligula theme. One of the works which made the greatest impact on Camus in his formative years was Grenier's collection of meditative and semi-biographical essays, *Les Îles*. In one of the essays, a particularly sensitive one called 'L'Île de Pâques', Grenier treats the theme of isolation and death ('ce fait aveuglant et écrasant de la mort') in a way that could not fail to appeal to Camus at this time. It is significant that this is one of the few essays to which Camus made specific reference in his preface to the 1959 edition of Grenier's book. It is in this essay that Grenier explains the title of the whole collection:

D'où vient l'impression d'étouffement qu'on éprouve en pensant à des îles? Où a-t-on pourtant mieux que dans une île l'air du large, la mer libre à tous les horizons, où peut-on mieux vivre dans l'exaltation physique? Mais on y est 'isolé' (n'est-ce pas l'étymologie). Une île ou un homme *seul*. Des îles ou des hommes *seuls*.[5]

The narrator describes his relationship with an invalid, a simple, uneducated man and very much 'un homme seul', being a paranoiac, who esteems his company for his enlightened conversation. The invalid senses that death may be imminent and tries to elicit the narrator's opinion about the possibility of life after death, evidently considering him a likely actuary of such metaphysical hazards ('vous qui avez fait des études . . .'). But the narrator hedges, for this is by no means his province: 'Je ne sais si le boucher s'en rendait compte: ce qui rendait possibles nos conversations à nous qui n'avions rien de commun, c'était une épouvante commune et quotidienne de mourir.' And in fact just as it has always been his own custom in the past to avoid such speculation by means of a heavy programme of reading, so he now tries to distract his friend: he brings him the *Lives of the Caesars* to read. The butcher is delighted. Having been thus distracted from mortal speculation by this macabre encyclopaedia of death he dies, and the essay ends on this ironic note. What is interesting is that Grenier alludes particularly to Caligula's crimes, and concludes: 'je ne goûtais guère que la couleur locale de ces histoires dont quelques-unes sont bien plus belles – *et n'en voyais pas le sens profond*.' This enigmatic attribution of significance where none would at first sight exist has subsequently been explained by Grenier: ' . . . j'ai dû en parler [de Suétone] plusieurs fois à Albert Camus en en faisant ressortir le sens nietzschéen de vies comme celles de Caligula.' In one of his earliest works, an 'Essai sur la musique', written shortly after he had come under the influence of Grenier in the *première supérieure* at the Lycée d'Alger, Camus was writing of Greek civilization in precisely Nietzschean terms, those of the *Birth of Tragedy*, which will find a direct echo in *Caligula* a few years later:

En effet, l'apollonisme et le dionysisme résultent du besoin de fuir une vie trop douloureuse. Les Grecs ont été déchirés par les luttes politiques, par l'ambition, par la jalousie, par toutes sortes de violences. Mais, direz-vous, il en est de même pour d'autres peuples? En effet. Mais par leur sensibilité et par leur émotivité, les Grecs ont été les plus aptes à la souffrance. Ils ont plus cruellement senti l'horreur de leur vie et ont été ainsi fatalement destinés au dionysisme barbare. De là le besoin de remédier à ces horreurs sauvages, en créant des formes ou plutôt des rêves, plus beaux que chez aucun autre peuple.

Et pour cela ils se sont servis de la danse et de la musique ...
(*Essais*, p. 1202.)

This immediately suggests a link between *Caligula* and 'le sens nietzschéen' which Grenier attached to the original Suetonius account. Camus's Emperor transforms himself into Venus, 'Déesse des douleurs et de la danse', and justifies himself with an argument which appears to be inspired directly by *Der Wille zur Macht*:

Tout ce qu'on peut me reprocher aujourd'hui, c'est d'avoir fait encore un petit progrès sur la voie de la puissance et de la liberté. Pour un homme qui aime le pouvoir, la rivalité des dieux a quelque chose d'agaçant. J'ai supprimé cela. J'ai prouvé à ces dieux illusoires qu'un homme, s'il en a la volonté, peut exercer, sans apprentissage, leur métier ridicule.

It is the failure of Hélicon to bring the moon which elevates Caligula to the truly Nietzschean plane of anagnorisis at the end of the play: 'Je n'ai pas pris la voie qu'il fallait, je n'aboutis à rien. Ma liberté n'est pas la bonne.' It remains for Caligula to shatter the mirror of delusion and be struck down by the mediocre, but relatively harmless, representatives of humanity. Some have interpreted the direction '*Cherea* [le frappe] *en pleine figure*' to indicate Cherea's loyalty in contrast with the treachery of the Old Patrician, who stabs Caligula in the back. Yet this is not altogether logical since it would have been just as loyal, and yet less brutal, for him to stab Caligula from the front *but in the body* instead of in the face. There is, I think, another reason for Camus's precise direction. Cherea's earlier remark to Caligula that 'on ne peut pas aimer celui de ses visages qu'on essaie de masquer en soi' suggests that there is rather a symbolic significance to this precise blow. Cherea, the true Dionysus-Apollo synthesis, shatters the mask of the false one, of the unbridled and self-deluding Dionysus which he himself might have become.

It is from this Nietzschean perspective that it is most appropriate to end this examination of *Caligula*. At the prompting of Jean Grenier, Camus has succeeded in turning a late Roman ragbag of prurience and propaganda into a tragedy which, relative to the transpositions of Cocteau, Giraudoux, Anouilh and the others, is more metaphysical, more primordial and – why not? – more Greek. *Caligula* is proof of the development that was made from the Théâtre du Travail to the succeeding company, and in every way indicates an appreciable maturing of Camus's art and thought. The massed workers of Oviedo, Prague and Algiers no longer fight over-simplified political and economic issues. Now, as we see with Caligula, Cherea and Scipion, there are no easy solutions. It is clear that in the evolution of Camus's politics and his theory and practice in the theatre, ethics and aesthetics are closely linked: 'In the "epic" theatre, therefore, there is no attempt to create fixed, highly individualized characters. Character emerges from the social function of the individual and changes with that function'[6] – Esslin's description suggests a reason for Camus's rejection of both Communism and the 'Communist theatre' of Brecht and Piscator. It was no more possible for Camus to subjugate his individualism at this time than at any other. Ultimately liberty was more important to him than justice. *A fortiori* the very dubious Communist notion of justice in Algeria between 1935 and 1937 could make no lasting hold on his allegiance. Likewise the future creator of some of the most individualistic characters of French literature in the middle of the century – Caligula, Meursault, Tarrou, Kaliayev, Martha,

Clamence – was ill suited, temperamentally, to both 'epic' and 'proletarian' theatre.

Just as Camus constantly asserted that *Caligula* had no overt political significance (although it is clearly a product of its age in a general philosophical sense), so the Équipe at this time, according to the manifesto of October 1937, would be 'sans parti-pris politique ni religieux'. A far greater flexibility and aesthetic pragmatism was proclaimed – and practised: '. . . la liberté la plus grande régnera dans la conception des mises en scène et des décors. Les sentiments de tous et de tout temps dans des formes toujours jeunes, c'est à la fois le visage de la vie et l'idéal du bon théâtre.' (*TRN*, p. 1690.) A far greater aesthetic and literary preoccupation is discernible. Camus's 'dégagement' from Communism is complete, and there is no obvious political bias in any of the five plays in the repertory (*La Célestine*, *Retour de l'Enfant Prodigue*, *Le Paquebot Tenacity*, *Les Frères Karamazov*, *Le Baladin du Monde Occidental*), or nine if one includes the envisaged productions of *Caligula*, *Othello*, *Les Esprits* and *La Comédie des Bagnes d'Alger*, to compare with that of *Le Temps du mépris* and *Révolte dans les Asturies*. Unlike the two anti-Fascist experiments, *Caligula*, as we have seen, possesses a totally ambiguous moral atmosphere, and is a much closer biographical reflection of the circumstances in which the play germinated. The inklings of ethical and meta-physical doubt which close examination revealed to be just below the surface of *Révolte dans les Asturies* now become the core of Camus's dramatic activity: 'Le Théâtre de l'Equipe . . . demandera aux œuvres la vérité et la simplicité, la violence dans les senti-ments et la cruauté dans l'action. Ainsi se tournera-t-il vers les époques où l'amour de la vie se mêlait au désespoir de vivre . . .' (*TRN*, p. 1690.)

It should now be clear why Camus preferred to regard the Théâtre de l'Équipe – the company for whom he originally wrote *Caligula* – as the real beginning of his mature theatrical career, rather than the Théâtre du Travail. By 1937 the first seeds of dis-illusionment were firmly implanted in Camus's sensibility. His first marriage had broken up, and he had been prevented by his serious ill-health from taking the *agrégation* and continuing with the university career for which he was so obviously suited intellectually. In Algeria the Communist concern for human justice had been revealed as a sham. In metropolitan France Blum's non-interventionist policy confirmed the inability of the Popular Front to assist the Spanish Republicans. Fascism marched onward in Spain, Italy and Germany. The present time was indeed for Camus one of the 'époques où l'amour de la vie se mêlait au désespoir de vivre'. *Caligula* is a crystallization of this experience. Camus's next play is written in even more despairing circumstances, and is situated in his contemporary world.

4 *Le Malentendu*

*Ainsi les hommes du Nord fuient aux rives de la Méditerranée,
ou dans les déserts de la lumière. Mais les hommes de la lumière,
où fuiraient-ils, sinon dans l'invisible?*

Camus, 1958 Preface to Grenier's *Les Îles*

Le Malentendu opened at the Théâtre des Mathurins on 24 August 1944, that is to say more than a year before the first performance of *Caligula*. Directed by Marcel Herrand, who also played the part of Jan, and with Maria Casarès as Martha, the play had two relatively short runs in 1944, neither of them particularly successful. The play works far less well than either *Caligula* or *Les Justes*, and has seldom been staged subsequently. Despite the order in which the plays were performed it is nevertheless appropriate to study *Le Malentendu* after *Caligula*. For not only was it written in its entirety some two years after the first drafts of that play, but it results from, and is a direct reflection of, experiences which can be clearly related to the years of gloom and despair which Camus spent in central France in 1942–3. If *Caligula* mirrors the nascent disillusionment of the late thirties, *Le Malentendu* consummates this disillusionment in terms which once again endorse the premisses of *Le Mythe de Sisyphe* and stress, even more than did *Caligula*, the inadequacy of its conclusions.

The play is quite different from *Caligula* theatrically. The anarchic vigour of *Caligula*, with its energetic chain of action, grimly amusing sketches, and fairly wide range of characters, tones and moods, finds no echo in *Le Malentendu*, which is austere in its plot and characterization and claustrophobic in mood. In an unused preface to the play Camus attributed the sombreness of *Le Malentendu* to his confinement in France during the black days of Vichy. He was exiled from that homeland to which, as is evident from almost every line he wrote about Algeria (except notably Oran), he was so deeply attached. He was cut off from his wife (he had re-married in December 1940), and from his friends and relatives. He appeared to be psychologically oppressed by his surroundings, being confined to le Panelier and le Chambon-sur-Lignon near Saint-Étienne in the landlocked Massif Central, which is different in almost every way from the Algerian coast of the Mediterranean. More menacing still was the political and military oppression and the risk of execution to which Camus, as a propaganda agent in the Resistance, was constantly subject. Finally, a renewed tubercular flare-up in the winter of 1942-3 exacerbated the author's mental depression. Evidence of the demoralizing effect of these circumstances abounds in the *Carnets* for this period, and helps to explain why *Le Malentendu* is commonly regarded as the blackest of Camus's works. And yet although conceding that the play breathes with the spirit of unhappy exile – it is dedicated nostalgically to 'mes amis de l'Équipe' – Camus asserted in this same preface and also subsequently that *Le Malentendu* should in no way be considered a work of despair. In the preface to the American edition of his collected plays (1957) he reiterated his claim that *Le Malentendu* is not entirely negative, and even contains optimistic implications. A claim which, as we shall see, is not easy to justify about a play which has as its theme the statement by the implacably embittered heroine who has just discovered that the man whom she has murdered is her own brother: 'c'est maintenant que nous sommes dans l'ordre – celui où personne n'est jamais reconnu.'

The plot of *Le Malentendu* has been summed up briefly by Camus in one sentence. It is about 'un fils qui veut se faire reconnaître sans avoir à dire son nom et qui est tué par sa mère et sa sœur à la suite d'un malentendu'. (*TRN*, p. 1729.) This immediately recalls a curious little episode in *L'Étranger*. In the second part of that novel Meursault, while awaiting trial for shooting the Arab, discovered an old piece of newspaper stuck to the underside of his mattress. It recounted a news item 'of which the first part was missing but which must have taken place in Czechoslovakia'. A young man left his village to seek his fortune.

C

Twenty-five years later he returned a rich man, accompanied by his wife and child. 'As a joke' he put up at the inn kept by his mother and sister who did not recognize him, and left his wife and child to stay elsewhere for the night. He made the mistake of showing his mother and sister how much money he had, and during the night they clubbed him to death, took his money and threw his body in the river. When his wife turned up next morning and revealed the identity of the victim his mother hanged herself and his sister threw herself into a well. Meursault concluded that the incident, which he read over and over again, was both improbable and natural. At any rate the victim rather deserved his fate: 'one should not play tricks'. This *fait divers* in *L'Étranger* is an example of the absurdity of the world and is as it were an oblique reflection of Meursault's own fate, since it anticipates his trial and conviction. The mother, not having been accorded enough 'recognition' according to the norms of the society which condemns Meursault, unconsciously avenges herself upon the son in the *fait divers* by not 'recognizing' him in turn. It is clear that Meursault is convicted and condemned to death less for murdering the Arab – he did so in self-defence after all – than for not weeping at his mother's funeral. He, like the Czech son, will die at least partly because of a breakdown in the mother-son relationship.

This news item is basically the plot of *Le Malentendu*. There are one or two minor changes. In *Le Malentendu* the returning couple have no child. This is possibly, as Quilliot suggests, because Camus wished to avoid pathos ('le pathétique de l'orphelin'), but more likely because he wished to concentrate on the bare essentials of the absurd situation, and the child has no relevance here (in any case a practical man of the theatre knows that child actors are a headache). Secondly, Jan in *Le Malentendu* is not clubbed to death but first drugged and then *drowned*; possibly once again, as Quilliot suggests, to avoid 'Grand Guignol', violent and bloody horror, but in any case the fate chosen by Camus helps to spin out the plot for three acts. As a result of one of the many 'misunderstandings' which give the play its title, Jan, by describing to his sister Martha the beauty of the country he has come from and which she hopes to escape to just at the moment when she is wavering in her resolve, causes her to reaffirm her natural intransigence. The middle of the second act is thus filled out with the process of serving Jan the drugged tea, once again as a result of an alleged 'misunderstanding' on the part of the simple-minded inn-servant. The short and frankly melodramatic Scene 5, in which Jan hesitates to drink and then does so with grimly ironic gusto ('Allons, faisons honneur au festin du prodigue!'), is followed by a far longer one between Jan and his mother who has decided at the last minute, *but just too late*, to prevent the guest from drinking the tea. Finally the significance of the drowning should not be missed. The river is the agent of his death, not just the repository of his dead body. As the source of both life and death, water has a constant poetic and symbolic force throughout Camus's work. It is significant that whereas she hanged herself in the *fait divers* the mother in the play throws herself in the river to be united in death with her son: 'A l'heure qu'il est, ma mère a rejoint son fils. Le flot commence à les ronger. On les découvrira bientôt et ils se retrouveront dans la même terre!' (*TRN*, p. 176.)

Details of the plot apart, the play diverges from the spirit of the *fait divers* in a fundamental philosophical way. In that curious anecdote the son decided to stay the night incognito 'par plaisanterie' – as a joke. It might have been a natural temptation for a playwright to make him the protagonist of a macabre black farce. But Camus's play has far more serious philosophical implications. *Le Malentendu* is not a *jeu d'esprit* about people who play tricks on the spur of the moment and find themselves imprisoned in the mask they have tried on when no one is looking, in the spirit of Pirandello and countless imitators. It is a highly subjective presentation by Camus of the human condition as he saw it in the desperate circumstances of 1942–3. In this respect it is important to notice that the tragedy is less that of Jan than of his mother, sister and wife. For much of the play Jan is not in the main focus, and the agony of these three women, the last of whom is completely innocent, is the prominent theme. And although not 'innocent' in the sense in which Maria is guiltless of any crime, even Martha and her mother may be said to be metaphysical innocents since they are the hapless victims of the absurd which poisoned their souls long before Jan decided to return. The play is a sustained metaphor of man's condition: one of sterility, exile and death in a world governed by the absurd: 'Quand les choses s'arrangent mal, on ne peut rien y faire.'

Camus's intentions are made clear by the fact that one of the earliest jottings for the play, and the first dialogued sketch, was the very last scene, surely one of the most totally despairing in modern theatre. This follows the long and brutal scene in which Martha has announced her intention of committing suicide once she has succeeded in disabusing Maria of 'l'idée que vous avez raison, que l'amour n'est pas vain, et que ceci est un accident. Car c'est maintenant que nous sommes dans l'ordre . . . celui où personne n'est jamais reconnu.' She exits with the injunction to her sister-in-law: 'Priez votre Dieu qu'il vous fasse semblable à la pierre. C'est le bonheur qu'il prend pour lui, c'est le seul vrai bonheur.' Maria is thus left alone, a pathetic figure, the last survivor of the main characters. The only other character in the play is the old servant, seemingly a deaf-mute who has shuffled on and off the stage enigmatically, and who will by now be far from the minds of nine out of ten people watching the play. But the short, shock confrontation lasting perhaps twenty seconds which closes the play was conceived by Camus from the very outset:

MARIA (*dans un cri*). Oh! mon Dieu! je ne puis vivre dans ce désert! C'est à vous que je parlerai et je saurai trouver mes mots. (*Elle tombe à genoux.*) Oui, c'est à vous que je m'en remets. Ayez pitié de moi, tournez-vous vers moi. Entendez-moi, donnez-moi votre main! Ayez pitié! Seigneur, de ceux qui s'aiment et qui sont séparés!

La porte s'ouvre et le vieux domestique paraît.

LE VIEUX (*d'une voix nette et ferme*). Vous m'avez appelé?

MARIA (*se tournant vers lui*). Oh! je ne sais pas! Mais aidez-moi, car j'ai besoin qu'on m'aide. Ayez pitié et consentez à m'aider!

LE VIEUX (*de la même voix*). Non!

RIDEAU.   (*TRN*, pp. 179–80.)

The character of the old man, completely grafted on to the *fait divers*, is the key to the interpretation of *Le Malentendu*. The working title used by Camus for the play when he drafted this scene was *Budejovice* (*ou Dieu ne répond pas*): the bracketed subtitle is an echo of Vigny's famous poem, 'Le Mont des Oliviers', in which Christ in his agony is presented as totally abandoned by his putative father. At the end of the first sketch for this scene Camus noted down the reminder 'Chercher les détails pour renforcer le symbolisme.' It is mainly through the character of the old servant that Camus does this. He speaks only the lines quoted above, and makes very few appearances during the course of the play. But these are very important appearances. One of the most symbolic is the one which anticipates Maria's experience in the last scene of the play. In Act 2 Jan feels himself overcome by his 'vieille angoisse' – 'je connais son nom. Elle est peur de la solitude éternelle, crainte qu'il n'y ait pas de réponse. Et qui répondrait dans une chambre d'hôtel?' He tries the bell in his room. The old servant comes, opens the door, stands motionless and silent, and goes away. Jan comments: 'La sonnerie fonctionne, mais lui ne parle pas. Ce n'est pas une réponse. (*Il regarde le ciel.*) Que faire?' In the first versions of the play, therefore, 'le Vieux', on the naturalistic level a taciturn old servant who seems to *misunderstand* and who shuffles round the inn without apparently doing much work, can also be taken because of his two appearances to Jan and Maria to symbolize the silence and indifference of God. But as Camus observed in the preface to the American edition,

il ne symbolise pas obligatoirement le destin. Lorsque la survivante du drame en appelle à Dieu, c'est lui qui répond. Mais c'est, peut-être, un malentendu de plus. S'il répond 'non' à

61

celle qui lui demande de l'aider, c'est qu'il n'a pas en effet l'intention de l'aider et qu'à un certain point de souffrance ou d'injustice personne ne peut plus rien pour personne et la douleur est solitaire.

In other words his role was ambiguous; quite naturally it caused disquiet in 1944.

In the revised 1958 edition of the play, however, Camus added or modified four very short incidents to transform the indifference of 'le Vieux' into something more sinister. Now Camus makes him direct Jan irrevocably along his suicidal course by means of crucial actions which are quite unaccountable on a literal level. In the opening scenes of the play the old servant is present when Martha and her mother are planning the crime and then again immediately afterwards when Jan is followed to the inn by Maria – he in fact hides from the latter pair so that they will not know that Maria has been spotted. He thus knows that Jan is going to be murdered and also that he is accompanied, but he does not inform his employers of this fact which would normally, of course, make the murder far too risky to be attempted. Shortly afterwards he even prevents Jan from being identified, for he enters apparently for no reason and distracts Maria at the very instant when she is about to check Jan's passport. She says, 'Non, je ne t'ai pas appelé,' and hands the passport back to Jan, having forgotten what she was about to do; she thus fails to discover that Jan has given her a false name. In the original version she had done this without any distraction from the old man, '[en pensant] visiblement à autre chose'. The revision seems to indicate an attempt on Camus's part to personify the working of the absurd and make it concrete on the stage.

This technique is applied with even greater force at the far more crucial moment when Jan has been drugged and his mother and sister are about to take his body to the river – the last possible moment when he could be saved. In the published 1944 and 1947 editions of the play Martha takes Jan's wallet from his jacket and counts the money. In the 1958 version this operation causes his passport to fall out of his pocket and slip behind the bed. The old servant prevents the women from discovering Jan's identity for the last time before he is murdered by removing the passport without being noticed. Once again there is no evident reason why he has done this, but, as the mother will say in Act 3 when she has discovered the truth: 'ce monde n'est pas raisonnable'. Finally, the fourth and last of these important modifications transforms the servant into the agent of Martha's and her mother's anagnorisis. This is once again by means of one of his seemingly unmotivated ten-second appearances. He simply enters, hands over the passport to Martha, and exits without a word or gesture. Camus's crisp stage direction for this action makes it clear that for him the character is now conceived quite differently from the doddery old servant in the early versions who had found the passport under the table *when urged by Martha to look for it.* One of the major paradoxes of the absurd for Camus was its banality, its manifestation in mundane details, hence this remarkably unhistrionic exploitation of anagnorisis, the traditional 'recognition of identity/realization of truth' scene, in *Le Malentendu*:

> *Martha ouvre le passeport et le lit, sans réaction.*

LA MÈRE. Qu'est-ce que c'est?
MARTHA (*d'une voix calme*). Son passeport. Lisez.
LA MÈRE. Tu sais bien que mes yeux sont fatigués.
MARTHA. Lisez! Vous saurez son nom.

> *La mère prend le passeport, vient s'asseoir devant une table, étale le carnet et lit. Elle regarde longtemps les pages devant elle.*

LA MÈRE (*d'une voix neutre*). Allons, je savais bien qu'un jour cela tournerait de cette façon et qu'alors il faudrait en finir.
(*TRN*, pp. 164–5.)

By means of this insidious symbolic figure of the old servant, therefore, Camus has sought to intensify the effect of unrelieved metaphysical blackness, culminating in the very last crushing syllable of the play: 'Non!'

We have already examined ways in which *Caligula* and *Révolte dans les Asturies* may be considered to be 'un champ d'observation pour le théoricien de l'Homme Révolté' (Robert de Luppé). *Le Malentendu* may in some respects be regarded as a companion piece to *Caligula*, although lacking the positive, Apollonian counterbalance of Cherea. Martha and her mother illustrate the anarchic instinct of those who, on perceiving the absurd (in their case, becoming aware of the awfulness of their Northern existence), react like Caligula by adopting a policy of rationalized destruction. The scale of destruction is, of course, considerably smaller, but, paradoxically, the metaphysical implications of *Le Malentendu* are more disturbing by an inverse proportion. Like Caligula, the murderers attempt to assume and perpetuate the absurd. They invent the same sort of justification for their crimes. Martha observes that their victims, who after all are drowned while unconscious, may be considered more fortunate than the wretches who throw themselves into the river with their eyes wide open, to which her mother replies:

> Quelquefois, en effet, je suis contente à l'idée que les nôtres n'ont jamais souffert. C'est à peine un crime, tout juste une intervention, un léger coup de pouce donné à des vies inconnues. Et il est vrai qu'apparemment la vie est plus cruelle que nous. C'est peut-être pour cela que j'ai du mal à me sentir coupable. (*TRN*, p. 119.)

which recalls Caligula's 'Si tu savais compter, tu saurais que la moindre guerre entreprise par un tyran raisonnable vous coûterait mille fois plus cher que les caprices de ma fantaisie.'

Caligula will follow out the 'logic to the very end', whereas Martha and her mother impose upon themselves a form of limit (just one more traveller will suffice to enable them to retire to 'the South') and also an ironical form of qualitative distinction, since they are selective and not arbitrary in their choice of victim. Despite these relatively mitigating circumstances, the message of *Le Malentendu* is more despairing than that of its predecessor. For whereas Gaius Caligula is at once the victim and the apotheosis of the absurd, which is thus, in its human form, shown to be vulnerable to human opposition, Martha and her mother never completely succeed in identifying themselves with the absurd. It remains beyond their grasp, to mock and crush them as implacably and ironically as they themselves crush Jan and Maria. Thus whereas the absurd in *Caligula* is embodied in a highly solipsistic aberration, in *Le Malentendu* it is presented almost as if it were a comprehensive malevolent force affecting in varying degrees all the characters in the play, and by implication the human race as a whole.

One of the most important themes is the impossibility of attaining personal happiness. Camus adapted the original anecdote by making Jan return to his homeland not just out of curiosity or in order to answer his family's needs, but because he himself feels a need. Despite his married happiness 'dans un pays que nous aimions, devant la mer et le soleil', something is missing: 'on ne peut pas être heureux dans l'exil ou dans l'oubli. On ne peut pas toujours rester un étranger. Je veux retrouver mon pays, rendre heureux tous ceux que j'aime.' He stays at the inn in the hope of being recognized by his sister and mother, particularly by the latter. More important than the literal meaning of this is the sense of being acknowledged and accorded a place in one's spiritual homeland: Camus will deal specifically with this difficult quest of the homeland or 'kingdom' in the six short stories grouped under the title *L'Exil et le royaume* in the 1950s. Maria believes that 'a mother always recognizes her son' and it is true that Jan's mother for some reason which she cannot explain instinctively recoils from this particular crime. But just as she is swept along by her daughter's will, so Maria is crushed by Martha's insistence that it is the natural order of things for 'no one to be recognized'.

Martha is embittered and warped beyond redemption. Her emotions are totally atrophied: 'J'entends mal les mots d'amour, de joie ou de douleur.' The setting of the play, Czechoslovakia – hence the working title 'Budejovice', a Bohemian town on the Moldau – is particularly important with regard to her character in so far as it forms part of the unfavourable half of the northern Europe–Mediterranean antithesis which informs all of Camus's work:

> Ah, mère! Quand nous aurons amassé beaucoup d'argent et que nous pourrons quitter ces terres sans horizon, quand nous laisserons derrière nous cette auberge et cette ville pluvieuse, et que nous oublierons ce pays d'ombre, le jour où nous serons enfin devant la mer dont j'ai tant rêvé, ce jour-là, vous me verrez sourire. Mais il faut beaucoup d'argent pour vivre libre devant la mer. (*TRN*, p. 117.)

Hers is the harsh existence of a friendless spinster in the chill northern world described by Camus in an essay of 1937, 'La Mort dans l'âme'. This essay, one of five in *L'Envers et l'endroit*, was based on Camus's own short, uneasy stay in Czechoslovakia, a country from which he moved with great relief to Italy, 'terre faite à mon âme'. Martha yearns for the spiritual relief – her fulfilment as a woman – which she believes to await her in the south. Sexually and emotionally frustrated, she is, as Quilliot has noted, 'like an intellectual obsessed by the flesh', and indeed has, as it were, read *Noces*: 'J'ai lu dans un livre que [le soleil] mangeait jusqu'aux âmes et qu'il faisait des corps resplendissants, mais vidés par l'intérieur.' (*TRN*, p. 120.)

Her misery is exacerbated by jealousy of her brother when the mother gives expression to her remorse for the murder. Martha goes so far as to claim that even if she had known their intended victim was her brother it would have made no difference. An 'unknown and indifferent' brother would be just like any other rich and unaccompanied stranger. Despite the basis of realistic social, economic and psychological motivation which Camus gives to Martha it would be wrong to attempt to interpret her character in purely naturalistic terms. Her yearning for the sun, the symbol of happiness and human fulfilment in the 'promised land', is seen to be as unrealizable as Caligula's quest for the moon. Jan's dissatisfaction with this Utopia, and migration back from the south to the north, points to the illusory nature of Martha's goal in the first place. Not for one minute should it be thought that Martha's and her mother's problem would be solved by the rediscovery of Jan and the acquisition of a husband and a Mediterranean villa. Camus simply has not written that sort of play. The fact is that the absurd has contaminated the existence of Martha and her mother – and by definition has done so irrevocably – long before Jan returns. They cannot escape any more than can Vladimir and Estragon in *En attendant Godot* or Garcin, Inès and Estelle in *Huis clos*. There is no exit.

Even less than we can visualize a transformed Martha being introduced by her brother to a bronzed male in the Club Méditerranée can we imagine the mother happily bouncing grandchildren on her knee on a family terrace in Provence. Even more than her daughter, she is consumed by a death-wish, in her case a physical and mental weariness that can find release only in religion or the grave. Once again, as with Martha, Camus supplies a few clues and then allows one to penetrate no further. The mother, like her daughter, is ostensibly worn out by a chill and harsh existence in an inhospitable country. A few passing allusions suggest that her past has been characterized by emotional sterility. When her son left home twenty years ago she did not embrace him. Her relationship with her husband was blighted by economic hardship: 'nous n'avions même pas le temps de penser l'un à l'autre et, avant même qu'il fût mort, je crois que je l'avais oublié.' When she tells Jan 'les vieilles femmes désapprennent même d'aimer leur fils. Le cœur s'use, Monsieur,' we realize that, desiccated and joyless old woman that she is, destined to murder her own son, the mother is in the last resort the most tragic figure in the play.

Yet it is through the fate meted out to the totally innocent Maria that the full force of Camus's pessimism comes across. It is interesting to note that in the first full draft of the play Maria's long and important scene with Jan in Act 1 did not exist. In the succeeding versions Camus wrote in this scene and also gave greater substance elsewhere to this completely sympathetic character, the embodiment of warm and tender femininity and uncomplicated sexuality. The writing of *Le Malentendu* was over-lapping with the reworking of *Caligula* at this time, and it is significant that Camus was thus filling out the character of Maria at about the same time he was adding greater weight (particularly dignity) to Cherea. Maria in fact was clearly developed by Camus to counterpoise Jan in the same way that Cherea became the focus for opposition to Caligula: she possesses Cherea's common sense, realism and strength of character. A serious defect in Camus's handling of this relationship in *Le Malentendu*, however, is that Maria does not exist on the same plane of reality – or rather unreality – as the other three main characters. Cherea understood the absurd and could speak the same language as Caligula in the end; Maria is totally uncomprehending. She is an outsider, incapable of understanding, even less of speaking, the hauntingly ironical and ambiguous mixture of literal and allegorical statement which is the language used by Jan, Martha and their mother throughout the play. From the aesthetic point of view this is perhaps a miscalculation on Camus's part. When, at the moment of truth in Act 3, Maria recoils and exclaims, 'Non, non . . . c'est moi qui suis folle et qui entends des mots qui n'ont encore jamais retenti sur cette terre. Je savais que rien de bon ne m'attendait ici, mais je ne suis pas prête à entrer dans cette démence. Je ne comprends pas, je ne vous comprends pas . . .' (*TRN*, p. 174) the temptation is irresistible for the audience to associate completely with the point of view of such a reasonable and sympathetic character. This is undoubtedly what happened when the play was first performed, and what will continue to happen. Contrary to what one might expect, therefore, Maria, far from helping the audience to 'get in' to this difficult play, serves only to keep it out, being an all too convenient repository and focus for confusion. It is not too far-fetched to suggest that the effect is rather as if, in *Caligula*, Camus had made Cherea even more sympathetic to the average audience than he is and yet at the same time as uncomprehending as, say, Caesonia or the First Senator. Cherea's vital role, in which he is assisted to a certain extent by Scipion, is to bridge the considerable philosophical gap between Caligula and the audience (the chorus, incidentally, does not have this explanatory function in *Caligula*, contrary to most assumptions; it is simply a ludicrous body intended to justify Caligula's rebellion without understanding its philosophical implications). Maria's failure to serve this function in *Le Malentendu*, despite the possibility that this was how Camus's artistic instinct intended to shape her, thus stems from the author's inability to integrate her into the play at the same philosophical level as the other characters. This is, I think, due to the fact that in the condition of total physical and spiritual depression in which he wrote *Le Malentendu* in the winter of 1942–3, Camus was even more closely involved with, and dominated by, the absurd than when he conceived and first drafted *Caligula*. The result is the impenetrable *démence* of Act 3. It is paradoxical that in this respect *Le Malentendu*, on the surface so austere in tone and stringent in structure and dialogue, is a much more emotionally charged, and less well-controlled, play than *Caligula*.

Conscious of the difficulties which *Le Malentendu* presents for interpretation and performance, Camus made two explanatory claims which he hoped would make the play more accessible. First he denied that the message of the play is totally nihilistic: on the contrary, he maintained, it propagates by implication a relatively optimistic message, an ethic of sincerity. In other words, everything would have worked out all right if Jan had not played tricks, if he had in fact done what his wife implored him to do, 'laisser parler son cœur'; if he had been straightforward and announced his true identity. This is a facile argument and would only work if *Le Malentendu* were centred upon Jan as the sole tragic hero who precipitates himself and his basically happy relatives into the abyss through *hubris*. For this to be true *Le Malentendu* would have to be a psychological tragedy, depicting the folly of an overweening ego. This it manifestly is not. We have already noted that Martha, who can make a good claim to being the central figure of the play, tells her mother '. . . si je l'avais reconnu, je sais maintenant que cela n'aurait rien changé.'

Camus's defence of the ethos he has created in *Le Malentendu* cannot stand up to the objection that he has presented the absurd as nothing if not all-pervading. The tragedy does not turn upon a personal or psychological issue, a defect of character in Jan or a clash between him and the other characters. The drab, rainsodden central European milieu, through the mists of which (as Maria points out) peer many unsmiling faces besides those of Martha and her mother, is a metaphor of the world as Camus saw it in 1942. The source of the tragedy is metaphysical, not psychological.

Camus's second statement, intending this time to account for the technical and aesthetic features of the play which caused alarm, was that *Le Malentendu* is an attempt at creating a modern form of tragedy. Now modern tragedy for Camus, as indeed for most twentieth-century dramatists who have tried to create it, would appear to be essentially metaphysical. It is not primarily a question of personality or psychology, of 'telling the truth'. Indeed as we shall see in Chapter 6 when dealing more specifically with Camus's theories of classical and modern tragedy, the author leans heavily on Nietzsche, not least in admiring the more cosmic tragedy of Aeschylus and Sophocles in preference to the psychological Euripides, the metaphysical in preference to the physical. And in fact Camus has striven to avoid naturalism in every aspect of *Le Malentendu*, in characterization, style of dialogue, dramatic form and setting. He provides the merest details to *situate* the characters and set the plot in motion. It is perhaps not altogether a coincidence that Meursault's scrap of paper related a news item *dont le début manquait*. The tragedy which Camus has based on it is likewise a story of which the beginning is missing. We have little or no idea of the characters' past or their psychological make-up, nor do we know the first thing about their appearance. Camus has stressed the general at the expense of the particular in exactly the same way with regard to the stage-setting and the Czechoslovakian milieu. The essential requirement is simply a cold, clean and sterile inn somewhere in the landlocked centre of Europe. No attempt whatsoever is made to particularize Czechoslovakia as such, which was chosen by Camus because as a student he had spent an unhappy stay in the limbo of impersonal hotel rooms in Prague (hence the malaise felt by Jan alone in his room in Act 2), and also no doubt because of his admiration for the work of Kafka with its unique evocation of loneliness, hallucination and nightmare. As far as the topography is concerned, however, the play might just as easily have been set in a landlocked province of Canada or Russia.

Now such neutrality as this is perfectly to be expected in classical tragedy. Camus in fact pointed out with regard to his dialogue, in which he deliberately contrived a corresponding effect of polished, articulate, non-colloquial discourse, that if he had dressed his characters in togas 'tout le monde peut-être aurait applaudi'. In the modern theatre, however, it is less easy for the average spectator to accept such anti-specific techniques in a play about the contemporary world. Camus has stripped the setting, action and characterization to the bare minimum, and yet still not succeeded in making us forget the modern world of passports, hotels and cups of tea, with or without drugs. The few material details are just enough to distract and disorientate. The same is true of the characterization. The few details which we glean about the sterile emotional relationships of the family in the past are just enough to provoke speculation of a psycho-sociological nature, and this dissipates the tragic tension which Camus is trying to create. The uneasiness felt by audiences since 1944 is due to the fact that they inevitably expect the deliberate ambiguities, tortuous verbal ironies and perplexing mixture of the symbolic and the literal in Act 1 to be succeeded by a clarification in the later course of the play, but this does not come. The ironies continue and the play becomes if anything more opaque. The improbabilities of the plot and the sheer lack of credible human attributes in the characterization become more and more obvious. Those who are not aware of the author's premiss that the world is absurd may take the play for a piece of derivative sub-Ibsen or early Anouilh naturalism. One might take the first six scenes of Le Malentendu as announcing Camus's contribution to the series of famous and highly theatrical 'amnesiac' plays, *Enrico IV*, *Sei Personaggi*, *Siegfried*, *Voyageur sans bagages*, *L'Inconnue d'Arras*, *Huis clos*, in which characters recall or relive a past from which, owing to amnesia, trauma, *mauvaise foi*, death or simply long absence, they have been cut off. But this is not a something-nasty-in-the-woodshed sort of play; there is no past to probe, there are no layers of illusion to peel away to reveal the 'truth': why Jan originally left home, what he hopes to find, what has *really* warped Martha.

Not the least remarkable feature of the perplexing familiarity, the spiritual *déjà vu*, which Camus has deliberately induced in the spectator or reader, is the haunting archetypal allusiveness of the central situation. I am not thinking so much of the ironic inversion of the parable of the prodigal son, to which in any case an overt reference is made by Jan, nor of the scores of extant folk-tales based on a similar or identical plot to that of *Le Malentendu*, as of other famous myths in which a son returns to his widowed mother and to a homeland which is a metaphor of evil and founders on the rocks of a defective parental relationship. But unlike Oedipus, Orestes or Hamlet, Jan has no discoveries to make about what really did happen to father, and who mother has been sleeping with ever since. The basic situation is de-sensationalized and de-dramatized by Camus for the reason that the absurd is undramatic and banal for most of the time. Jan passes sleepily and politely into oblivion ('Je voudrais du moins vous remercier,' he yawns to his mother) half-way through the play, not at the end of it after any Aristotelian anagnorisis: such is the quiet but lethal working of the absurd. In strictly classical terms *Le Malentendu* has no beginning, not much of a middle, and even less of an end. The twentieth-century equivalent of the truth about Oedipus is that father died of overwork and mother has worn herself to the bone in private partnership with her daughter ever since. It is an irony which would have pleased both Gide and Cocteau.

It may seem strange to talk of the anti-Aristotelian and anti-theatrical character of a play which has been much praised for its unified plot and relentless linear progress to a climax, but my feeling is that *Le Malentendu* is in one or two important respects closer to the world – and theatrical style – of Ionesco, Adamov, Buzzati and Frisch than has been realized. Of course it is legitimate to apply traditional dramatic criteria to *Le Malentendu* (and they reveal many defects), but it is just as fruitful to consider how close the play comes to making the imaginative leap of form and structure from what Esslin calls the rational and discursive school (Camus and his contemporaries, Sartre, Anouilh, Giraudoux, Salacrou, etc.) to the 'Theatre of the Absurd'. Much of the difficulty which *Le Malentendu* always presents for performance stems from the fact that it is an uneasy compromise between *Huis clos* and *Voyageur sans bagages* on the one hand and plays like *Le Professeur Taranne*, *Tueur sans gages*, *The Fireraisers* and Buzzati's *Un Caso Clinico* on the other. In the first place Camus moves further than any of his 'Cartesian' contemporaries towards resolving the fundamental paradox which the absurd will always present in modern literature: how can an artist communicate to his audience his conviction that it is impossible for human beings to communicate? *Le Malentendu* is precisely about the lack of understanding between those in whom it should be easiest, mother and son, husband and wife, brother and sister. The latter pair in particular, Jan and Martha, engage in long verbal duels, double-meanings-at-five-paces. Their ironies are conscious or unconscious, but the absurd sees to it that each character blindly ignores that element of what his interlocutor either insinuates or concedes which would bring about the double recognition: for Jan the realization that his mother and sister intend to kill him; for the women the realization that the man they intend to kill is their kinsman. D. M. Church, in an otherwise excellent analysis of this whole process, compares, inappropriately I think, the atmosphere of these scenes to that of the 'recognition scenes' in Euripides' *Electra*. He quotes Friedrich Solmsen:

[In the Euripides play] the whole pattern of this episode is a movement toward the desired event, then away again, then there is another turn which takes us closer and closer, almost infinitesimally close to what we expect in great suspense, and this is again followed by a movement away from this point. The same pattern occurs in several other plays of Euripides, always employed . . . for a recognition that might and should materialize but does not. There is always this arising of hopeful chances, words are spoken that might lead to the discovery; [there is] always the same picture of humanity, of men or women so intent on finding what they desire, striving and struggling so desperately for it, and [who] when they are face to face with their happiness [and] would only have to reach out and grasp it . . . are blind.[1]

Church concludes: 'These words could very easily have been written about *Le Malentendu*. In this attempt to create a modern tragedy Camus remains close to the traditions of the ancient Greek variety.' Now although one takes Solmsen's point, and Church's, about the common ground of desperate striving on the part of characters who in the last resort prove to be blind, the dramatic movement and the atmosphere of the two plays in these scenes are quite different. In the first place the scene in *Electra* is, as Solmsen states, an *episode*, and it is furthermore one which produces, or is intended to produce, *great suspense*. *Electra* is not specifically a play about the impossibility of recognition and communication. The scene referred to is a piece of 'theatre' (in a sense which Camus would consider pejorative), a suspenseful episode, a piece of orthodox dramaturgy, the sort of effect which he is capable of producing in his plays, as we shall see in *L'État de siège* and *Les Justes*, but which he does not seek for its own sake. The corresponding scene, or rather scenes, in *Le Malentendu* are altogether more subtle technically and aesthetically. The ambiguity and cross-purpose which Camus creates in the numerous scenes between Jan and his mother, and Jan and Martha particularly, are philosophical themes far more than suspense-provoking devices, and they are exploited thematically throughout the play, not episodically. In the Euripides, Orestes knows all along that the peasant girl he has met is Electra, and the dramatic irony of the ensuing confrontation is all at her expense. The misunderstanding is entirely one-sided. In any case it is ended ere long by one of those wise old tutors with a good memory for tell-tale scars, specially taken down off the shelf and dusted by Euripides for the purpose. In *Le Malentendu* the balance of reciprocal misunderstanding and non-recognition is essentially even. On the one hand Jan knows that his hosts are his mother and his sister but not that they are going to murder him; they do not know that the man they are going to murder is the son and brother who wants more than anything to bring them happiness. This creates a macabre double-irony which can be appreciated only by the audience and which is far more complex than the frankly rather naïve dramatic irony which Euripides' audience must share with Orestes (not forgetting Pylades at the usual discreet distance). In Camus's play, then, one detects a totally different atmosphere, as though the very pattern of dialogue with its ebb and flow of double meanings is animated by a satanic presence constantly steering the tragic trio away from the obvious. In other words Camus is attempting to make the language itself a metaphor of the absurd, and comes very close indeed to achieving that fusion of form and content which characterizes the best of the Theatre of the Absurd only a few years later. The significance, finally, of Camus's modification of the role of 'le Vieux' should by now be clear. It is important to recall that it was not until the television versions of the 1950s and the revised stage version of the play in 1958 that this took place, that is to say until after the Theatre of the Absurd had made its initial impact and Camus had adapted Dino Buzzati's *Un Caso Clinico*. It is not improbable that Camus was encouraged by the new ideas about dramatic form which prevailed in the French theatre after 1950 to exploit this latent affinity of *Le Malentendu* with the Theatre of the Absurd in a way which would have been quite foreign to him in 1943. If, as Quilliot suggests, Camus was considering a completely new version of his play at the time of his death, it is tempting to suggest that he would have tried to secure the artistic redemption of *Le Malentendu* by further progress in this direction.

5 L'État de siège

Le XVIIe siècle a été le siècle des mathémathiques; le
XVIIIe celui des sciences philosophiques et le XIXe celui de
la biologie. Notre XXe est le siècle de la peur.

Camus, 'Ni victimes ni bourreaux'

Quand une fois la liberté a explosé dans une âme d'homme,
les Dieux ne peuvent plus rien contre cet homme-là.

Jupiter in Sartre's *Les Mouches*

There can be little doubt that *L'État de siège* is the most ambitious
of all Camus's plays – and the most unsuccessful. It opened on
27 October 1948 'dans les ors et velours du Marigny, devant un
Tout-Paris irrémédiablement futile', but failed to live up to the
promise held out by the collaboration of such prestigious figures as
Barrault, Renaud, Casarès, Brasseur, Bertin, Marceau, Desailly,
Honegger and Balthus (the latter pair being responsible for the
music and décor respectively). The critics on the whole understood and sympathized with the message of the play, a passionate
endorsement of man's duty to rebel against political tyranny, but
complained of lifeless characterization, pretentious verbiage,
puerile symbolism and incomprehensible balletic *mise en scène*. In
Camus's own words, 'certainement, il y a eu peu de pièces qui
aient bénéficié d'un éreintement aussi complet'. (*TRN*, p. 1730.)
It is thought that Camus resented the fact that Jean-Louis Barrault, the director and leading actor of the production, with whom
he had spent a whole year creating the play, took it off so soon
after the initial poor reception. But Barrault has made it clear that
the cost of maintaining such an expensive production in the hope
of an eventual recovery was prohibitive.

Several critics laid most of the blame for the play's failure at
Barrault's door. They alleged that he had induced Camus, by now
regarded as one of the leading literary figures of the post-war

period, especially after the acclaim accorded to *La Peste* a year earlier, to write in a style which was alien to his temperament and talent. The extent to which Camus may have been adversely affected by the forceful personality of Barrault during the long period of 'collective creation' of the play is difficult to assess. Camus's *Carnets* are no help whatsoever in this respect (and in fact they illuminate *L'État de siège* in general to nothing like the same extent that they do the other three plays). The fact nevertheless remains that Camus has not distributed blame for the failure, and has accepted complete responsibility for the published text. This latter fact alone entitles us to examine *L'État de siège* as an expression of his thought and art at a given time with even greater confidence than was the case with *Révolte dans les Asturies*, parts of which are definitely known to have been written by his collaborators.

Reference to *Révolte dans les Asturies* is appropriate in more than one respect. Like that first collaborative effort in which Camus was involved, *L'État de siège* is a drama of rebellion in a Spanish provincial town, this time Cadiz instead of Oviedo. Like *Révolte dans les Asturies*, too, it is an experimental work making use of some of the same agit-prop techniques, and placing a great reliance on aggressive sound and lighting effects and choreography. But here the comparison ends. The statistics and documentary propaganda of Piscator, and the fervently left-wing and anti-bourgeois satire of Brecht, combined to dramatize a specific event, are now behind Camus. The target of the rebellion in *L'État de siège* is much more generalized: it is totalitarianism in all its forms, right-wing and left-wing. The dictatorship against which Diego, the new version of Pèpe, will rebel is a synthesis of Stalinism, Nazism and Italian and Spanish Fascism. Direct allusion to specific personalities of contemporary politics is now replaced by allegory, and statistics give way to a highly ambitious poeticism. Camus in fact stated that his preference for an allegorical style was due to his desire to capture something of the spirit of medieval French morality plays and more particularly of the Spanish *autos sacramentales*, the extremely successful genre which propagated Catholic dogma on religious and profane issues right up till the eighteenth century.

The play is divided into three parts. The first contains a prologue in which disaster is presaged for the peaceful city of Cadiz by the dramatic appearance of a comet in the night sky. Despite the warnings of the police and of the judge Casado, the citizens are confirmed in their fears for their future by the iconoclastic ironies of a drunken nihilist, appropriately named Nada. He is challenged by Diego, a young medical student engaged to Casado's daughter Victoria, who encourages the citizens to resist the temptation of fatalism: 'Que vous importe? Gardez votre coeur ferme et ce sera assez.' The prologue closes with a clear social pattern emerging: the judge, the Civil Guard and the Governor (via his herald) symbolize complacent, authoritarian, middle-class rule in a classic pre-revolutionary society, one in which an illiterate and superstitious peasantry is easily manipulated by the priesthood, by politicians or by other external forces. How is this society to react to the approaching calamity, the exact nature of which is as yet unknown? By trusting in the conservatism of the traditional establishment (Casado), rushing headlong into intellectual despair and nihilism (Nada), or by lucid and courageous resistance (Diego)? In his American Preface Camus frankly pleaded guilty to 'all charges of creating symbolic characters in this play'.

The remainder of the first part shows the city capitulating to the calamity: it is the plague. The Governor, judge, priest and leaders of society can offer no effective resistance; Diego organizes medical relief. It is at this stage that the play becomes much more overtly allegorical. A bulky, uniformed man, Plague, accompanied by his lady secretary Death, takes over the city, deposes the Governor and presses the First Alcalde into service as a puppet ruler. Death possesses a directory of all the inhabitants' names; she causes those who resist to be stricken with the plague by the simple process of striking their name off the list with her pencil. Nada however is spared because 'celui-ci a le genre qui ne croit à rien et . . . ce genre-là nous est bien utile'. The interrelationship of this allegorical trio is important for Camus's thesis. Plague stands for totalitarianism (and, as I shall attempt to show, a particular sort). Plague has as his faithful servant Death: totalitarianism attains and maintains power through murder. Plague is welcomed by Nada: totalitarianism is propagated by embittered and nihilistic intellectuals and succeeds where there is also popular predisposition to defeatism.

In a series of edicts the dictator establishes censorship, curfews, rationing and the compulsory denunciation of all citizens known to be afflicted with the plague. The gates of Cadiz are closed, and the city is now, like Oran in *La Peste*, in a state of siege. Part 1 closes on Plague's long harangue to the citizens. He intends to banish 'la ridicule angoisse du bonheur, le visage stupide des amoureux, la contemplation égoïste des paysages et la coupable ironie. A la place de tout cela, j'apporte l'organisation.' Organization and reason will now govern their whole existence. Instead of dying as they used to, peacefully or by accident or as a result of an explosion of uncontrollable passion, at any rate *à l'espagnole*, they will now die, as they will live, *methodically*: 'vous aurez vos fiches, vous ne mourrez plus par caprice . . . je vous apporte le silence, l'ordre et l'absolue justice.'

The first half of Part 2 deals with the regimentation of the citizens in a series of grimly comic sketches satirizing bureaucracy gone mad. Nada willingly assists Plague and Death:

NADA. Oui. Ça t'humilie, donc c'est bon. Mais revenons à ton commerce. Préfères-tu bénéficier de l'article 208 du chapitre 62 de la seizième circulaire comptant pour le cinquième règlement général ou bien l'alinéa 27 de l'article 207 de la circulaire 15 comptant pour le règlement particulier?

L'HOMME. Mais je ne connais ni l'un ni l'autre de ces textes!

NADA. Bien sûr, homme! Tu ne les connais pas. Moi non plus. Mais comme il faut cependant se décider, nous allons te faire bénéficier des deux à la fois.

L'HOMME. C'est beaucoup, Nada, et je te remercie.

79

NADA. Ne me remercie pas. Car il paraît que l'un de ces articles te donne le droit d'avoir ta boutique, tandis que l'autre t'enlève celui d'y vendre quelque chose.

L'HOMME. Qu'est-ce donc que cela?

NADA. L'ordre!   (*TRN*, p. 245.)

Diego tries to organize resistance but is forced to flee, leaving behind him a cowardly and humiliated citizenry who whine: 'L'autre court! Il a peur et il le dit. Il n'a pas sa maîtrise, il est dans la folie! Nous, nous sommes devenus sages. Nous sommes administrés.' Diego takes refuge in Victoria's house, but her father wishes to deliver him over to Plague 'because it is the law': 'Je ne sers pas la loi pour ce qu'elle dit, mais parce qu'elle est la loi. DIEGO: Mais si la loi est le crime? LE JUGE: Si le crime devient la loi, il cesse d'être crime.' Diego in his despair and demoralization seizes the judge's young son as a hostage and threatens to infect him with the plague if Casado makes a move to betray him. He has now sunk to the level of his enemy: 'rien n'est lâche dans la cité des lâches.' Victoria prevents him from carrying out his threat. He flees once more, and she accompanies him. Diego's action in releasing the boy hostage and deciding instead to risk his life in the hostile world outside, even though his capture would certainly reduce the city's chances of overthrowing Plague, is thus the characteristic decision of the true rebel, and has a parallel in *Les Justes*. In ordinary human terms Diego has realized, like Kaliayev, that the life of an innocent child is too high a price to pay for the hypothetical freedom of a far greater number of people. In the strictly personal terms of Camus's philosophy of revolt he has reached that vital *limit* beyond which rebellion becomes revolution.

Victoria now has a rival in the form of the lady secretary Death who hints to Diego: 'la fatigue me rend sentimentale. Avec toute cette comptabilité, des soirs comme ce soir, je me laisse aller.' Diego rejects her advances in a passionate tirade. When Death laughs in his face Diego strikes her, and the men of the chorus utter a great cry of release. Death informs Diego that, in conquering his fear, he has discovered the weakness in Plague's system. The message bears a striking likeness to that conceded by Jupiter in Sartre's *Les Mouches*. Death tells Diego: 'il a toujours suffi qu'un homme surmonte sa peur et se révolte pour que la machine commence à grincer. Je ne dis pas qu'elle s'arrête, il s'en faut. Mais enfin, elle grince et, quelquefois elle finit par se gripper.' The act ends as the breeze from the sea, the symbol of Cadiz's freedom, begins to blow once more.

In Part 3 Diego organizes effective resistance to Plague, and incites the citizens to overcome their fear and to rebel. Faced with imminent defeat, Death and Plague play one of the last cards in their hand. Death hands her directory to the citizens who thus seize the opportunity to liquidate their personal enemies – a clear allegory of the grim *règlements de comptes* which were carried out in France during both the Occupation and the Liberation (and which frequently had nothing to do with the specific crime of collaboration). The carnage is stopped by Diego, now supported by some of the citizens. Plague's last card is his hostage – Victoria, stricken with the plague. He offers her to Diego in exchange for the city. Diego refuses the offer: 'L'amour de cette femme, c'est mon royaume à moi. Je puis en faire ce que je veux. Mais la liberté de ces hommes leur appartient. Je ne puis en disposer.' Plague admits that his bluff has been called. If Diego had agreed to the exchange all would have been lost, Diego, Victoria and the city. Now Plague is forced to accept Diego's original offer of his own life for Victoria's. Even Death rebels in the end against Plague's systematization of her function, annihilation: 'J'étais libre avant vous et associée avec le hasard. Personne ne me dé-testait alors. J'étais celle qui termine tout, qui fixe les amours, qui donne leur forme à tous les destins. J'étais le stable. Mais vous m'avez mise au service de la logique et du règlement. Je me suis gâté la main que j'avais quelquefois secourable.' Plague departs, content for the moment with the life of Diego, and taking satis-faction from the fact that the old guard are returning to the city. Their stupidity and complacency are sure to give him an oppor-tunity to strike again in the future. Perhaps next time there will be no rebellion: 'Ce jour-là je régnerai vraiment dans le silence définitif de la servitude.' Perhaps next time there will be no one like Diego who is prepared to sacrifice his life, his love and his innocence. As Diego dies the chorus of women, echoing Maria in *Le Malentendu*, bewail their eternal fate. It is to be left behind by their menfolk in their quest of the absolute, whether it be the frenzied pursuit of political idealism, of total organization of human resources (which can thus be perverted to totalitarianism) or, as now with Diego, the attainment of integrity, or rather redemption of integrity in death. As the wind of liberation blows once more over Cadiz from the sea, Nada, in a last cynical diatribe, also hails the return of the old guard, whose first action is to distribute decorations and honours among its members. He then throws himself into the sea: 'Je sais trop de choses, même le mépris a fait son temps. Adieu, braves gens, vous apprendrez cela un jour qu'on ne peut pas bien vivre en sachant que l'homme n'est rien et que la face de Dieu est terrible.'

A complex plot, involving the full range of Camus's political and philosophical themes. Initially some confusion reigned about the relationship of *L'État de siège* to *La Peste*. A superficial resemblance – a port being cut off from the outside world by an incursion of the plague, actually allegorized in the play by a character named la Peste – not unnaturally at the time led some to believe that the play was a free adaptation of the novel. Camus denied this, and in fact it was hardly necessary for him to do so since there are so many different characters, themes and symbols – completely inverted in function in the case of the wind from the sea, for example – that *L'État de siège* may be considered a completely separate and independent work from *La Peste*. And yet seen in the context of Camus's evolving thought, the play and the novel are partly complementary. The link between them needs to be explained if *L'État de siège* is to be fully understood.

It is commonly accepted that *La Peste* is not satisfactory as a symbolic (even less as an allegorical) representation of the German occupation of France. Its inadequacy is indicated by the numerous and important gaps in the frame of reference to the real situation of France in 1939–45. The war was not a conflict between men and an inscrutable non-human force which disappears as mysteriously as it comes, nor was the camp of the victims united. There is no parallel situation in La Peste to represent the demoralizing conflict between Vichy and the Resistance. The petty profiteer Cottard has his reasons for welcoming the plague but he does not on his own symbolize the not inconsiderable proportion of the French population who supported Vichy and the collaboration for both practical and ideological reasons. He is a marginal figure, in no way constituting a threat to the resistance offered by Rieux, Tarrou and the others. Not all of the men and women who collaborated with the Nazis were crooks and opportunists: some, no doubt misguided in their political calculations, believed with great sincerity that they were saving French lives while waiting for a better chance to strike back. This whole element of political ambiguity is lacking in La Peste. Again, how could a symbolic representation of the Occupation, however stylized, fail to examine the key issue of reprisals and the intense moral dilemma in which it placed the men of the Resistance? It was the existentialist situation par excellence as every decision had to be assessed on its merits. Every assault on German men and materials was certain to provoke the execution of innocent compatriots; hence nightmare equations had to be made. What was in the greater interest of the French people at any given time: to blow up a German ammunition train and possibly (but not certainly) bring German defeat a step nearer, or to conserve the lives of the dozen or more French citizens who would be executed simply because they lived in the nearest village to the act of sabotage? Who was to say when the price was too high?

The answer is the ordinary man, the one who by joining the Resistance automatically accepted responsibility for his own actions, even though his civilian background had in no way prepared him for this existence of intense moral anguish. The psychological stress which men like Grand and Rambert undergo in La Peste by agreeing to continue to fight alongside Rieux and Tarrou is in no way comparable. The essential element of moral ambiguity which would have been provided by the possibility that on occasions the *équipes sanitaires* might have to sacrifice the lives of innocent citizens of Oran is lacking. So too, and more important, is the possibility that the plague owed its origins to a group of power fanatics, aided and abetted in general by certain classes of citizen. These were the principal objections of those left-wing critics in 1947 who denounced *La Peste* as a totally inaccurate allegory of the Occupation and Resistance. They were right up to a point. Far from stressing what would appear to be the lesson of the war, the conventional enough literary theme of *homo homini lupus*, Camus showed the man of his age to be devoured not by the wolves of the Wehrmacht, the Gestapo, or the *milice*, but by an evil of unknown origin. In so far as man is seen by Rieux in the last chapter of the work to be susceptible throughout all time to such a scourge, the work represents a generalization of the human condition. Like *Le Malentendu* in this respect, it was planned and partly written while Camus was sequestered in central France:

> Je veux exprimer au moyen de la peste l'étouffement dont nous avons tous souffert et l'atmosphere de menace et d'exil dans laquelle nous avons vécu. Je veux du même coup étendre cette interprétation à la notion d'existence en général. La peste donnera l'image de ceux qui dans cette guerre ont eu la part de la réflexion, du silence – et celle de la souffrance morale. (*Carnets* 2, p. 72.)

Thus Camus intended *La Peste* to be at one and the same time a picture of man's metaphysical condition and an allegory of the Occupation. As such the work is the fulcrum between *Le Mythe de Sisyphe* and *L'Homme révolté*. *L'État de siège*, on the other hand, looks forward quite definitely to the latter work, and was created in an atmosphere which was very different from that in which *La Peste* was conceived. Now Camus appears to heed the criticism of *La Peste* that the 'bourreaux' should be named. By 1948 Camus was considerably disillusioned by the turn that political events had taken since 1944: the escalation of the Cold War, the failure of the French press, including *Combat*, to achieve independence from commercial and political interests, the restoration of the same sort of repressive economic and industrial system which was responsible for much of the instability of the later years of the Third Republic, the vicious retribution meted out to collaborators, and the use of torture and excessive force to suppress insurrection in the Sétif and Kabyle regions of Algeria in 1945 and in Madagascar in 1947 – all this experience had affected Camus's sensibility by the time he was working on *L'État de siège*. He was convinced that it was not until these post-war years that France sank to the nadir of moral degradation – 'la dernière et la plus durable victoire de l'hitlérisme – ces marques honteuses laissées dans le cœur de ceux-mêmes qui l'ont combattu de toutes leurs forces'. (*Essais*, p. 314.) The evidence of the *Carnets* and Camus's journalism from 1944 to 1947 shows that he was becoming less and less averse to recrimination as his disillusionment increased. In these circumstances it is not surprising that he should have accepted Jean-Louis Barrault's offer to collaborate on a 'total spectacle', based on the latter's original plan for a play about the purgative role of the plague, which would allow him to express his own misgivings about contemporary France and Europe. The result was to be 'un mythe qui puisse être intelligible pour tous les spectateurs de 1948'. (*TRN*, p. 187.)

One of the principal weaknesses of *L'État de siège* stems from Camus's and Barrault's failure to work out clearly in advance the exact dramatic form this myth would take. It so happens that for some time before they knew each other Camus and Barrault were both attracted by the theme of the plague as purgation, and by the philosophical implications of trial by evil generally. With Camus this theme found expression in *La Peste*. Barrault for his part endeavoured to write a play based on Defoe's *Journal of the Plague Year*, which Camus himself used as one of his principal sources. The dramatic possibilities of this theme were suggested to Barrault by Artaud whose *Théâtre et son double* he considered to be 'incontestablement ce qui a été écrit de plus important sur le théâtre au XXe siècle'.[1] As a young actor and director at Dullin's Atelier at the time of Artaud's performance of *Les Cenci* in May 1935, Barrault was so taken with Artaud's revolutionary concept of the theatre as to offer his services in partnership with Artaud. The offer was declined but Barrault was to retain nothing but the greatest respect for the author of 'Le Théâtre et la peste' and the other articles which appeared periodically in the middle thirties before being published under the collective title *Le Théâtre et son double* in 1938. Although of course not acquainted with Artaud, Camus shared this awareness of his work in the 1930s. The manifesto of the Théâtre de l'Équipe in fact refers to 'la violence dans les sentiments et la cruauté dans l'action' – an allusion no doubt to one of Artaud's articles, 'Le Théâtre et la cruauté'. The first clear internal influence in Camus's work, however, is to be found in *Caligula*, where the emperor's pestilential nihilism appears to have been directly inspired by 'Le Théâtre et la peste'. At the height of Caligula's campaign of terror Cherea pinpoints an important mitigating feature of Caligula's cruelty – some might say its complete justification:

> Reconnaissons au moins que cet homme exerce une indéniable influence. Il force tout le monde à penser. L'insécurité, voilà ce qui fait penser. Et c'est pourquoi tant de haines le poursuivent.

And shortly afterwards Caligula himself formulates this interpretation of his role as the purger of men's illusions and mendacity, in precise Artaldian terms:

> Mon règne jusqu'ici a été trop heureux. Ni peste universelle, ni religion cruelle, pas même un coup d'État, bref, rien qui puisse vous faire passer à la postérité. C'est un peu pour cela, voyez-vous, que j'essaie de compenser la prudence du destin. Je veux dire . . . je ne sais pas si vous m'avez compris (*avec un petit rire*) enfin, c'est moi qui remplace la peste.

The superficial appeal of Artaud for Camus is obvious. At a time when he was deploring what he considered to be the effete badinage of Giraudoux, Artaud held out hope of a return to fundamental human – or rather, inhuman – experience in the theatre. Artaud wanted the theatre to be a paroxysm, an explosion of terrifying, subterranean forces. Guicharnaud has compared the delirium he wished to create to Rimbaud's *dérèglement*, and considers his contribution to modern theatre 'to lie not so much in form itself, but in a basic intention: a theatre of shock intended not to awaken the public to current problems but to use them or go beyond them in revealing man's metaphysical reality, hard as it may be to take'.[2] Artaud, interpreted literally, could hardly inspire a whole corpus of dramatic literature of a sort which would appeal permanently to Camus, since he advocated a complete ban on discursive dialogue and its replacement by a synaesthetic language – lights, moving shapes, sounds of all sorts, incantatory vocalization, mime and gesture. Camus, on the other hand, clung instinctively to words, characters and reason. Nevertheless, before *L'État de siège*, he had already written at least one play, *Caligula*, which, in its ends if not in its means, breathed with much of the spirit of Artaud. Even *Le Malentendu*, although owing less obvious a debt to Artaud, being formally static and conventional – a good example of the 'théâtre dialogué' which Artaud abhorred – conveys by means of the insidious, robot-like character le Vieux and the supernatural conclusion a powerful and highly personal vision of metaphysical reality.

There is on the other hand a gulf between these two plays and *L'État de siège* which, from the formal point of view, may well have been created with Artaud's theories in mind. Guicharnaud's distinction between 'current problems' and 'metaphysical reality' is important because I think it shows where Camus and Barrault went wrong in using Artaud's theme as a 'myth for 1948'. Whereas in *La Peste* the plague symbolized the evil which lurks in men's souls like rats in dark corners, in *L'État de siège* the character Plague, dressed in Nazi uniform, stands unmistakably for totalitarianism. Artaud on the other hand detested the explicit: 'pour moi les idées claires sont, au théâtre comme partout ailleurs, des idées mortes et terminées.' Artaud could not have been more anti-verbal; *L'État de siège* is overloaded with dialogue. The failure to seize upon the essential features of Artaud – a shock montage of light, sound and movement to evoke supernatural forces of evil independent of humanity, and a strict avoidance of contemporary issues – was total.

There can be no doubt that in *L'État de siège* the socio-political plane of allusion gains the upper hand over the metaphysical. Whereas in *La Peste* the *pestiférés* were the innocent victims of a somewhat abstract expression of the absurd, in *L'État de siège* they are the (frequently deserving) victims of its concrete and human manifestations. Far from being an expression of inscrutable hazard – the sort that triggered off disaster by unaccountably taking Drusilla from her brother or by distracting Martha from checking Jan's passport at the crucial moment – the absurd is now shown to be of human origin, expressed in human tyranny, and consequently vulnerable to human resistance. Camus makes this point several times in the play. That it is a question of human, rather than superhuman or divine or abstract, injustice is stated clearly by Nada as soon as the comet appears:

Ai-je parlé du ciel, juge? J'approuve ce qu'il fait de toutes façons. Je suis juge à ma manière. J'ai lu dans les livres qu'il vaut mieux être le complice du ciel que sa victime. J'ai l'impression d'ailleurs que le ciel n'est pas en cause. Pour peu que les hommes se mêlent de casser les vitres et les têtes, vous vous apercevrez que le bon Dieu, qui connaît pourtant la musique, n'est qu'un enfant de chœur.

And once the dictatorship has been established the chorus cries at the end of Part I: 'Qui me délivrera de l'homme et de ses terreurs?' Diego at first sees the evil as absolute and metaphysical: 'Mais la douleur est dans ce ciel qui pèse sur nous!' but Victoria, in an outburst which recalls Maria's condemnation of man's quest of the absolute in *Le Malentendu*, exhorts him to accept that all human beings are to some extent imperfect, and that the only viable solution to the problem of the relative guilt of mankind is to aim at relative victory. She counters Diego's claim to be fighting 'l'injustice qui nous est faite' by stressing that he should regard as his enemy 'le malheur qui est en toi'. At the end, when Diego and human solidarity triumph over Plague and Death, Diego formulates the political lesson of the play: '. . . aucun homme n'a assez de vertu pour qu'on puisse lui consentir le pouvoir absolu.' *L'État de siège* is very much a play about absolute power, and takes the form of a sweeping broadside aimed at the many spheres of European life – political, social, religious, economic – in which a misuse of power was considered by Camus to be a cause of human degradation in the 1940s. There are several different frames of satirical reference.

To begin with, the manner in which Plague captures Cadiz suggests certain features of the German occupation of France and other countries in the war. The complacency of the population ('le monde mais pas l'Espagne') is matched by the head-in-the-sand attitude of their leaders, and rewarded by a rapid abdication of official leadership and resistance by the Governor. The dramatization of this incident is crudely satirical:

> Dans votre intérêt même, il convient peut-être que je laisse cette ville à la puissance nouvelle qui vient de s'y manifester. L'accord que je conclus avec elle évitera sans doute le pire et vous aurez ainsi la certitude de conserver hors de vos murs un gouvernement qui pourra un jour vous être utile? Ai-je besoin de vous dire que je n'obéis pas, parlant ainsi, au souci de ma sécurité, mais . . .

A puppet leader is easily pressed into service ('c'est un grand honneur'); collaboration is obtained without too much difficulty, and panic, looting, black market, fratricidal betrayal and mistrust are soon rife among the population. There is ample indication that Camus found post-war developments in France even more disquieting from the human point of view than the war itself.

D

When the citizens are given the chance to carry out their own 'éliminations' by means of Death's notebook, they do so with relish, squaring private accounts and at the same time wreaking brutal vengeance on black-marketeers and collaborators. This recalls Camus's claim in 1945, when a fourteen-year-old child launched a savage attack on a lynched collaborator, that it was not until Nazism was defeated that its tyranny over France was consummated: 'à la haine des bourreaux a répondu la haine des victimes.' Even Diego is degraded temporarily, and Victoria is repulsed by his 'visage de peur et de haine'. Finally the old guard establishment returns, and the fact that a contemptuous reception of them is entrusted to a character who is himself contemptible, Nada, does not veil the extent to which it is a reflection of the author's own disgust on seeing his hoped-for reform of public life fail to materialize after the war. Shortly before, Death, another unlikely repository of Camus's sentiments, rails at the ordinary people of the town for their apathy towards revolution. Her cynical tirade, although inconsistent with the anti-Communist, and by implication anti-revolutionary, trend of thought which starts with this play and culminates in *L'Homme révolté*, is nevertheless a reminder that Camus had been in favour of revolution in 1944-5 and had not hesitated to use the word in its accepted sense. The slogan of the Resistance newspaper *Combat* throughout the war was 'De la Résistance à la Révolution'. Finally the dénouement, depending on the fate of a hostage, Victoria (as well as the earlier incident when Diego seized Casado's son), stresses that element of moral ambiguity and human sacrifice which one would consider to be an indispensible part of any fictional treatment of the Second World War in occupied France.

Leaving aside contemporary allusions, we see that the play contains a considerable amount of traditional anti-bourgeois and anti-clerical satire. Camus derides the established forces of society in a more virulent and comprehensive way than in any other of his works. The Governor and the alcaldes, the judge, priest and police are portrayed as eminently corruptible, hypocritical and blindly reactionary ('rien n'est bon de ce qui est nouveau'). Perhaps not surprisingly in a play containing so many characteristics of the epic – just like *Révolte dans les Asturies* in fact – the satire is somewhat lacking in subtlety: 'Du reste, et pour le moment, la maladie s'attaque surtout aux quartiers extérieurs qui sont pauvres et surpeuplés. Dans notre malheur, ceci du moins est satisfaisant' announces the First Alcalde to 'murmurs of approval'. Judge Casado in particular, one of many judges in Camus's work who are the target of contempt, is a Brechtian caricature of bourgeois vileness. He incarnates intransigent legalism, immorality and religious hypocrisy of the sort which backs up faith in God with careful contingency planning. 'Le Seigneur est mon refuge et ma citadelle,' he intones, a few seconds after telling his wife to hoard all the supplies she can lay her hands on. Throughout, the priest is a figure of cant and cowardice and bears more resemblance to an ubuesque caricature then to Paneloux in *La Peste*, whom Camus portrayed with compassion although not sharing his interpretation of evil.

It is not difficult to account for the gusto and vehemence of this anti-establishment satire. As a result of his influential position after the war and the degree of security afforded him by the sales of his books, Camus ran the risk of any successful artist or intellectual of humble origins, namely of being taxed with 'embourgeoisement'. In an important series of articles entitled 'Ni Victimes ni Bourreaux', published in *Combat* in November 1946, Camus attacked Marxism in general and the Soviet Union in particular because of the disquieting information coming out about the Stalinist dictatorship. These articles appeared to justify charges that Camus had forsaken his early left-wing intransigence, and a Marxist intellectual, Emmanuel d'Astier de la Vigerie, virtually accused Camus of being a crypto-Capitalist and 'fils de bourgeois' all along. In two open letters Camus defended himself of charges of being in alliance with the bourgeoisie and stressed his opinion that the Western capitalist régimes, buttressing Franco and conniving at the liquidation of Communists in Greece, were just as loathsome to him as Soviet dictatorship in Eastern Europe.

L'État de siège, with its broad satire of bourgeois attitudes and institutions, may therefore be regarded as a dramatized *third* 'Réponse à Emmanuel d'Astier de la Vigerie'. By means of the heavy satirical dosage Camus was seeking, as it were, to put the record straight and also obviate further attacks on his anti-Communism of the sort which had just been made. At the same time it was a chance to widen the range of the spectacle by making an aunt sally of what had been traditionally an easy target in the French theatre. Barrault's artillery could be relied upon to be well primed for the task.

Even so, it is doubtful that *L'État de siège* could have afforded d'Astier de la Vigerie and friends any more satisfaction than did 'Ni victimes ni bourreaux' since, for all its anti-bourgeois zeal, it is just as profoundly an anti-Communist play by implication. It is true that many of the techniques of repression used by Plague's régime are the familiar ones of bureaucratic fantasy and mystification which one associates with the work of Capek, Kafka and Brecht and which here have a National Socialist ring. For example, the systematic humiliation of interviewees at the beginning of Part 2 recalls a similar interrogation scene in Malraux's *Le Temps du mépris*, which, it will be remembered, was adapted and produced by Camus for the Théâtre du Travail in 1936. It is true also that in Barrault's production Plague wore a Nazi uniform. On the other hand there is no parallel in the play to the racialism, perfervid nationalism and paranoia, and ceremonial and cultural mystique which must have figured prominently in French memories of Nazi Germany in 1948. On the whole the principal manifestations of Plague's tyranny suggest rather that Camus was attempting to evoke the rigid Procrustean spirit of dialectical materialism in its most forbidding form, that of Stalinist Russia. Gadourek's report that Camus would have preferred Plague to be dressed as an impeccable civil servant is significant. 'Je vous apporte le silence, l'ordre et l'absolue justice' – these are the conditions which, as Camus was to assert in detail in *L'Homme révolté*, constitute the goal of northern historicism. This 'beau système qui ne laisse rien au hasard' relies blindly on a mid-nineteenth-century determinism which claims that 'on peut tout expliquer dans une société bien organisée'. Everything can be codified, rationalized and controlled, even death and 'le néant' if necessary. Universal destruction need be no handicap: 'La ville sera rasée et, sur ses décombres, l'histoire agonisera enfin dans le beau silence des sociétés parfaites.'

The character Plague embodies an ideology which posits the subservience of man to the dialectical process, and this theme dominates the play. L'État de siège, to all appearances a potpourri of political and social polemics, is principally, but by no means solely, an attempt to create an anti-Marxist myth. Not surprisingly, when one considers the hypersensitivity of French political and intellectual circles, by trying to keep everyone happy Camus succeeded in pleasing no one. The left were less gratified by the satire of the right than provoked by the parody of dialectical materialism. The converse is equally true of the right wing, who objected to the Spanish setting. Gabriel Marcel claimed to speak for 'all those who feel strongly about human dignity and freedom' when he argued that the play ought to have been set on the coast of Yugoslavia or Albania rather than in Cadiz.[3] Camus's reply comes closer than anything else he wrote to explaining his aims in the play. With the retort 'Pourquoi Guernica, Gabriel Marcel?' Camus opens his defence by pointing out that it was in Spain that the totalitarian régimes first tried out their strength. He denounces the subsequent collusion of France and other countries in Franco's suppression of republicanism. He also defends his sporadic but pointed satire of the Roman Catholic clergy: he had given the church an odious role because that was precisely what it had played during the Civil War. Camus's final argument in his reply to Marcel is surely a good one, and it is still valid twenty years later. If the West wishes to reserve the right to denounce totalitarianism in eastern Europe it cannot afford to undermine its whole moral position by accepting allies who are Fascist dictators: '. . . la tyrannie totalitaire ne s'édifie pas sur les vertus des totalitaires. Elle s'édifie sur les fautes des libéraux.'

Unfortunately the success of a play is seldom directly proportionate to the ethical purity of the author's motives for writing it. The fact is that the play was a resounding failure in Paris in 1948, and has not had a professional revival anywhere in French. The production apparently had much to do with it. The reaction of Jacques Lemarchand, Camus's ex-colleague on *Combat*, was typical of those critics who were all the more disappointed after the first night for being totally in sympathy with the political and social arguments of the play, yet so unimpressed with it as theatre:

> Nous attendions les éclats de cette vive colère, de cette indignation juste et profonde qui sonne dans toute l'œuvre de Camus. Et il y a dans *l'État de siège* tous les éléments nécessaires à ce *Mariage de Figaro* que notre époque attend. Les formules dramatiques, celles que nous voulions entendre, sont là. Elles sont régulièrement noyées dans ces sonneries de sirène, ces doux mugissements Martenot, ces piétinements de foule réglée, ces beaux changements d'éclairage, qui distraient l'attention, l'éparpillent – pourquoi?[4]

Camus in fact designated the play a *spectacle*, one intended to combine many elements of dramatic expression, mime, chorus, farce, choreography and musical accompaniment. The spectacular aspect and technical virtuosity of Barrault's production appear to have created problems of a practical nature. François de Roux complained of not having heard 'une phrase entière dite par Maria Casarès'. A production in which Maria Casarès of all people cannot be heard is obviously defective.

But leaving aside technical considerations of what went wrong in 1948 the fact remains that for the spectator, as for the reader twenty years later, the play is impenetrable on a human level. René Barjaval was just as unconvinced as Lemarchand by the characterization, particularly of the crucial figures of Diego and Victoria:

> Jamais, jamais, au long de ces trois actes interminables, jamais une réplique simple, humaine, un cri du cœur ou de la chair,

jamais un soupir de vie. Même lorsque les deux amants sont face à face et se disent leur amour et leurs souffrances, au moment de se quitter, de se retrouver ou de mourir, jamais nous n'entendons l'amour ni la souffrance, mais des mots, des mots, des mots . . . Et lorsque le chœur parle de l'été, de l'hiver, des fruits, nous ne sentons ni le froid, ni le chaud, ni l'odeur du verger, mais seulement celle de la poussière.[5]

The most damning opinion came from Pierre Quemeneur:

La cause du désastre me paraît inhérente au génie même de l'auteur. (Et je pense à Camus plus encore qu'à Barrault.) Je ne crois pas que Camus ait le don de démiurge. *Il me paraît marqué d'une étrange impuissance à créer des personnages.* (My italics.)[6]

The root of the trouble is that amid the massive display of allegory and propaganda there is no human focus. Diego and Victoria in particular are virtually puppets, only too obviously exemplifying Camus's evolving philosophy of limits. They are not credible as human beings and are given to mouthing statements – John Cruickshank aptly calls them 'parallel speeches [which] fail to make contact' – in an inflated pseudo-poetic style which on occasions sounds like pastiche Claudel, or Corneille at one huge remove, such as that of being translated into English and back again into French with the alexandrines missing. These two characters could have saved the play, in the same way that a completely convincing central figure or relationship reconciles us to the propaganda and conscious distancing techniques of Brecht. Maria Casarès had the unenviable task of delivering the following lines, with the bathos of 'Terre' two-thirds of the way through:

Ah! ne parle pas ainsi, pour l'amour de nous, ou je vais tomber devant toi et te montrer toute ma lâcheté. Car tu ne dis pas vrai. Je ne suis pas si forte. Je défaille, je défaille, quand je pense à ce temps où je pouvais m'abandonner à toi. Où est le temps où l'eau montait dans mon cœur dès que l'on prononçait ton nom? Où est le temps où j'entendais une voix en moi crier 'Terre' dès que tu apparaissais. Oui, je défaille, je meurs d'un lâche regret. Et si je tiens encore debout, c'est que l'élan de l'amour me jette en avant. Mais que tu disparaisses, que ma course s'arrête et je m'abattrai.

To which Diego replies: 'Ah! Si du moins je pouvais me lier à toi et, mes membres noués aux tiens, couler au fond d'un sommeil sans fin!' Death interrupts them and asks them, 'Que faites-vous?', to which Victoria shouts 'L'amour, bien sûr!' But no one can have been convinced. Diego's task is no easier. He is a paragon of a virtue, limited rebellion, and outside the allegorical characters, Death, Plague and Nada, there is no character in Camus's theatre who is more obviously intended to embody preconceived philosophical ideas. Diego's speciality is the one-line moral recommendation, either of virtue in general or of what he has just done or is about to do in particular. At another time, in another dramatic convention, and above all in another poetic form, Corneille found the *formule juste* for the hero's confident self-appraisal: 'Je suis jeune, il est vrai; mais aux âmes bien nées/La valeur n'attend point le nombre des années.' But what was splendid bombast in Don Rodrigue now rings hollow in Diego, the twentieth-century symbolical medical student: 'Je suis content de mourir, Victoria. J'ai fait ce qu'il fallait.' Some of his utterances are so priggishly *boy-scout* as to make one think that perhaps Nada has a point after all:

Ne blasphème pas, Nada. Voilà déjà longtemps que tu prends des libertés coupables avec le ciel.

C'est une sottise! Mentir est toujours une sottise.

Personne n'est au-dessus de l'honneur.

Mourir n'est rien. Mais mourir souillé!...

The moral rhetoric reminds one, too, of German *Sturm und Drang* and Romantic drama, and it is interesting, to say the least, that *L'État de siège* in German translation is reported by Raymond Gay-Crosier among others to have had 'un succès remarquable' in Germany, Switzerland and Austria.[7]

The ostentatious virtue of Diego – when demonstrated by dialogue such as this – makes it very difficult to believe in him as a twentieth-century everyman. He is a crude cardboard cut-out labelled The Hero (Ideal Rebel) whose every action embodies an aspect of *L'Homme révolté*, nowhere more so than in the long middle section where, suddenly inconsistent with his general character, he threatens the life of the judge's son and then reverts to the honourable course. Nothing has prepared us for this double volte-face. Camus has not succeeded in convincing us that this is what Plague does to people. If anything the comedy and farce of the bureaucratic satire and the wit and irony of Plague and Nada militate against the atmosphere of contagious terror which is meant to evoke the experience of living under an increasingly pervasive totalitarian régime.

The transparency of the characters of Diego and Victoria is matched by an irritating over-simplification of most of the other characters. The representatives of middle-class morality are corrupt and contemptible right from the start. If Camus wishes to make a point about the ludicrous ease with which this state of affairs allows totalitarianism to take over the city, then it is not clear how. Nor is the exact relationship between Plague and Nada, totalitarianism and nihilism, made quite explicit enough for 'un mythe qui puisse être intelligible pour tous les spectateurs de 1948'. Nada, surely, ought to have been far more influential in the city *before* the arrival of Plague and Death, since nihilism for Camus is a direct contributory factor to totalitarianism rather than merely its servant once it has been established. And is it as simple as all that to overthrow totalitarianism? As far as the hard facts of twentieth-century politics are concerned, *L'État de siège* ultimately leaves the most important questions unanswered. Then again, when Death tries to 'seduce' Diego, is this meant to allegorize the temptation of suicide – a key theme from *Sisyphe* to *L'Homme révolté*? As the incident is handled, it would seem not. It is very brief: the Secretary, Death, tells Diego that she is attracted to him and 'la fatigue me rend sentimentale. Avec toute cette comptabilité, des soirs comme ce soir, je me laisse aller.' Diego's reaction is limited to the characteristic line: 'Je préfère votre haine à vos sourires. Je vous méprise.' One is left with the suspicion that there is here the germ of an interesting philosophical idea which Camus failed to expand in practice with Barrault. So the incident passes rapidly in the theatre at a literal level, so rapidly in fact that even those members of the audience who were fully familiar with *Le Mythe de Sisyphe* would need to have more than an average share of wits about them to grasp the allusion, if one is intended. The framework of allegorical reference is in fact constantly breaking down, so that in the last resort the play is not strictly speaking allegory but a hotchpotch of characters and sketches, some of which are totally symbolic, others literal. There is an irreconcilable gulf between the requirements of particularized socio-political polemics on the one hand, and the nakedly moralistic generalizations of the *autos sacramentales* on the other.

6 Les Justes

Tous les crimes ne me déplaisent pas également.

Jupiter in Sartre's *Les Mouches*

Les Justes opened on 15 December 1949 at the Théâtre Hébertot, just over one year after the failure of *L'État de siège* at the Marigny. In a letter to a M. Germain on 13 February 1950 Camus considered the play to have been 'chaleureusement accueilli par les uns . . . froidement exécuté par les autres. Match nul par conséquent.' (*Essais*, p. 1627.) Despite the author's pessimistic interpretation of the initial critical reaction, the play turned out to be a victory for Camus and enjoyed a run of over 400 performances. Theatre critics have on the whole been less enthusiastic about the play as theatre than academic critics, many of whom would share John Cruickshank's view that the play is Camus's 'greatest dramatic achievement'. To my mind the play lacks the passion and spontaneity of *Caligula*, being an avowedly didactic drama about the limits of political terrorism, but it can nevertheless produce some extremely powerful moments in the theatre. It is an astringent, tightly controlled attempt at modern tragedy. In its style and structure it follows the baroque extravaganza of its political and philosophical companion-piece *L'État de siège* in the same way that the black austerity of *Le Malentendu* complemented the theatricality of *Caligula*. These two plays were a highly personal presentation of the 'sensibilité absurde' and of the reaction which this condition can provoke: revolt. But the revolt of Caligula and Martha was a false revolt because expressed at the expense of other people. Together with *L'Étranger* and *Le Mythe de Sisyphe* they formed what Camus called the cycle of 'négation'. *Les Justes* on the other hand is relatively more constructive and didactic, as is, more explicitly, *L'État de siège*, and thus forms part of Camus's second cycle, that of 'le positif', together with *L'Homme révolté* and, less obviously, *La Peste*. This cycle is positive in that it represents what Camus considered to be the only justifiable revolt against the absurd: one which will be exercised at the expense not of other people but of the self. All four works are in varying degrees didactic, and, in the broadest sense of the term, political, in dealing with the relationship between the individual and society.

Like *L'État de siège*, *Les Justes* is about rebellion against tyranny, and it was intended by Camus to possess a relevance to contemporary European politics. But whereas *L'État de siège* was a curious blend of allegory and particularity, a generalization of Fascist and Stalinist totalitarianism in the mid-twentieth century, *Les Justes* is in the essentials of its plot historical and specific. It is centred upon the assassination in Moscow in 1905 of the Grand Duke Sergei Alexandrovitch, the uncle of Tsar Nicholas II. The hero of the play is the man who threw the bomb, the student and poet, Ivan Kaliayev. Kaliayev held back at the first attempt on seeing that the Grand Duke was accompanied by his nephew and niece, Dimitri and Maria. Two days later, however, the Grand Duke was alone and Kaliayev killed him. He made no attempt to escape, was arrested, tried and executed. All this happens off-stage in *Les Justes* and is spread over five acts. Almost all of the play is set in the room which the small band of assassins have rented, the exception being Act 4 which takes place in Kaliayev's cell the day after the assassination, when he is visited by the Chief of Police and the widowed Grand Duchess.

If the enactment and/or narration of this historical event along documentary lines were the sole purpose of *Les Justes*, Camus would have had to pad out the plot by including large chunks of reconstituted data about the assassination and the personalities of the assassins, and the socio-political background. Such historical material is, however, kept to a strict minimum. The language and material reality of the play are highly stylized. The 1950 edition of the play eliminates a number of precise details of the assassins' existence, techniques and preparations which had existed in Camus's draft of 1949. This is once again a characteristic feature of his style: the constant search for an almost classical French degree of abstraction and the excision of all extraneous anecdotal and topical material, of all, in fact, which might blur the focus of the crucial dramatic issue. To this end Camus stressed that he did not regard *Les Justes* as a historical play as such. His purpose was different. What he has done is very interesting. He has interpolated into the historical situation a central conflict between Kaliayev and a co-terrorist named Stepan Fedorov. This conflict serves both an artistic and a philosophical purpose. It is of the greatest possible relevance to Camus's anti-Marxist polemics of the period 1945–51, and at the same time it is the essential structural antagonism upon which is based his attempt to create a modern tragedy: 'J'ai essayé d'y obtenir une tension dramatique par les moyens classiques, c'est-à-dire l'affrontement de personnages égaux en force et en raison.' In Act 2 Stepan, who stands out from the rest of the group as a brutal realist (having been embittered by years of emprisonment under the Tsarist régime), criticizes Kaliayev vehemently for the failure of the first attempt, that is to say for not having a strong enough stomach to throw the bomb into the coach despite the unexpected presence of the two children. He believes these children should have been sacrificed for the freedom of the serfs. This failure means that months of preparations have been wasted and the group is once again in peril of being tracked down by the fearsome Okhrana with their task undone. Kaliayev finds such a policy morally repugnant; the end does not justify the means. In this he is completely supported by the three other members, Dora, the leader Annenkov, and Voinov. They counter Stepan's attack with the powerful argument that the assassination of children would in any case prove counter-productive by alienating potential supporters of the revolution. Far more than this, however, it is the intrinsic ethical issue which is at stake – a very important point. I propose to examine the exploitation of this central conflict between Kaliayev and Stepan Fedorov at some length, because it seems to me that no play more than *Les Justes* illustrates the difficulties Camus experienced in reconciling the rival claims of the artist and the moralist.

Many accounts of *Les Justes* appear to be based on an implicit acceptance of the play as a reasonably successful modern tragedy. The heroic, exalted atmosphere, particularly that generated by the sacrificed love of Kaliayev and Dora, is much admired, and comparisons are made with *Polyeucte* and *Le Cid*. But just as in Corneille's theatre the border-line between tragedy and tragicomedy is frequently in dispute, so in *Les Justes* the author's moral ardour can be sensed to be in such an uneasy relationship with his artistic judgement that one is roused to question the play's claim to being tragedy. I doubt whether it is this so much as a type of theatre which Camus considered distinctly inferior – melodrama. In a lecture on 'L'Avenir de la tragédie' delivered in Athens in 1955 Camus pronounced unequivocally on the distinction between tragedy on the one hand and 'le mélodrame ou le drame' on the other: tragedy is the clash of two irreconcilable forces, equal in power and legitimacy, whereas in melodrama only one of the forces is justifiable. Tragedy for Camus is antithetical tension which must not be broken by stressing one element at the expense of the other. Whereas Romantic theatre, and melodrama in general, pit goodness against evil (and frequently in absolute quantities), true tragedy must represent a conflict characterized by ethical ambiguity. Neither of the antithetical terms must be an absolute, or possess a monopoly of virtue:

. . . les forces qui s'affrontent dans la tragédie sont également légitimes, également armées en raison. Dans le mélodrame ou le drame au contraire, l'une seulement est légitime. Autrement dit, la tragédie est ambiguë, le drame simpliste. Dans la première chaque force est en même temps bonne et mauvaise. Dans le second, l'une est le bien, l'autre est le mal (et c'est pourquoi de nos jours le théâtre de propagande n'est rien d'autre que la résurrection du mélodrame). Antigone a raison, mais Créon n'a pas tort. De même Prométhée est à la fois juste et injuste et Zeus qui l'opprime sans pitié est aussi dans son droit. La formule du mélodrame serait en somme: 'Un seul est juste et justifiable' et la formule tragique par excellence 'Tous sont justifiables, personne n'est juste.' (*TRN*, p. 1703.)

Clearly, if he judged his own theatre by these criteria, Camus can have had few illusions about *L'État de siège* by 1955; *Les Justes* is a different matter. He strove to establish and maintain a tragic equilibrium between two antagonists who can both support their policies with sound practical and moral arguments. The success of the play as tragedy will thus to a large extent depend on Camus's ability to sustain this tension through to the dénouement.

The two other principal prerequisites of tragedy which Camus stressed in Athens are particularly relevant to the political and philosophical subject-matter of *Les Justes* even more than to Camus's other plays. The first is a classical Greek concept which has been much appreciated as an artistic and philosophical formula for tragedy in France, probably more than in any other western European theatre. It is the indispensability of *mesure* in human conduct, or, to use the terms which echo throughout Camus's works, the importance of observing 'la limite qu'il ne faut pas dépasser'. Caligula's campaign was 'un jeu qui *n'a pas de limites*...la récréation d'un fou'. The mother in *Le Malentendu* would like Jan to be the last victim; she does not know that they have already gone beyond the limit. In *L'État de siège* Diego is led at one stage to argue that there are no limits in the fight against Plague-Tyranny. The boy's life can be taken if necessary because 'rien n'est lâche dans la cité des lâches', but the message of the play eventually is the chorus's cry that 'il n'y a pas de justice, mais il y a des limites'. In *Les Justes* Camus is asking: what is the limit to the violence one can commit in the pursuit of just ends? To what extent is one justified in descending to the level of brutal and unscrupulous enemies if there is no other means of bringing about justice and democracy? In other words, does a totally desirable objective for the mass of mankind justify such an extreme act of *démesure* as political assassination, and, if it does, how can this *démesure* be atoned for? Secondly, and very important, where does the killing have to stop? If the only way to remove a tyrant is to kill a child at the same time, does not the 'rebellion' forfeit both practical and ethical value? In fact even if the tyrant alone is killed does not the rebellion, in Camus's terms, automatically become 'revolution'?

The second characteristic of tragedy as defined by Camus in Athens in addition to the problems of moral equilibrium is more controversial and raises the whole question of tragedy as an artistic and philosophical phenomenon. Tragedy, according to Camus – and few would disagree with him here – has flowered only twice, and briefly on each occasion: in Athens in the fifth century B.C. and in western Europe during the late Renaissance – the age of Marlowe, Shakespeare, Corneille, Racine, Lope de Vega and Calderón. Somewhat echoing the theories of the nineteenth-century German dramatist Hebbel, which in turn were an application to the theatre of the dialectical theories of Hegel about the individual and the evolution of the state, Camus sees both ages as being periods of transition and upheaval. An age of faith and 'mystery' was being challenged and replaced by an age of reason and individualism. The ideal tragic climate was the point at which the balance of forces was even, whereupon the representative of the new order, the tragic hero, rose up 'en contestation avec l'ordre divin, personnifié dans un dieu ou incarné dans la société'. Camus suggests that Aeschylus' *Prometheus Bound* reflects the ideal tension, the ideal balance of forces in an age of transition. While divine order triumphed there could be no tragedy, either before Aeschylus or before the Renaissance. The converse is equally true: that once divine order was subordinated to the various social and political manifestation of humanism tragedy was equally impossible. 'La tragédie athée et rationaliste est donc elle aussi impossible. Si tout est mystère, il n'y a pas de tragédie. Si tout est raison, non plus. La tragédie naît entre l'ombre et la lumière, et par leur opposition.' Although Camus took *Prometheus Bound* as his model of the tragic situation in so far as it pitted a symbol of rebellion against his former masters, the gods, Camus proclaims Sophocles to be the tragic dramatist *par excellence* among the ancients because his tragedies were centred upon the crux of the historical transition and did not resolve the conflict totally in favour of either of the two terms. The counterpart to Sophocles in western European tragedy is Shakespeare. Euripides was the culmination of the Greek tragic movement, and, so Camus implies, an inferior tragic dramatist because he disturbed the balance in favour of psychology and the individual. His modern counterpart is Racine: 'Racine et la tragédie française achèvent le mouvement tragique dans la perfection d'une musique de chambre.'

The disadvantage of such a schematic survey in a reasoned case for the feasibility of modern tragedy – not to mention the questionable implication that Racine was automatically inferior to Shakespeare because less cosmic and metaphysical – is obvious. By drawing an exact parallel between Greek and western European drama Camus appears to preclude all possibility of a recurrence of tragedy in our time. If nothing came after Euripides why should anything come after Racine? It is at this stage that Camus parts company with Hegel, Hebbel, Nietzsche and all the others who have demonstrably influenced his analysis of the tragic phenomenon. He enters on new and disputable territory in claiming that the climate is equally suitable for tragedy in the twentieth century. At first sight all the evidence would appear to be against this. After the French Revolution the rebel triumphed over the pre-existing order, which was Christian feudal or monarchic society. In theory at least, the spirit of Prometheus and Socrates, Faust and Descartes, reigns supreme; there is no established order of terror and mysticism to provoke rebellion. What therefore in the twentieth century will be the modern forms of order versus rebel to constitute the antithetical terms of modern tragedy? Camus's answer is that the modern tragic hero-rebel will not be a later version of the Renaissance figures, taking on the same forces as Faustus. Those battles have been won. For Camus, it is the liberators themselves, the spiritual descendants of Descartes and Saint-Just who have become the tyrants. In *L'Homme révolté* Camus adapts the tragic archetype Prometheus as his symbol of the modern rebel who transgresses the limit between rebellion and revolution, and is thus transformed from the champion of mankind into a dictator:

> Ici s'achève l'itinéraire surprenant de Prométhée. Clamant sa haine des dieux et son amour de l'homme, il se détourne avec mépris de Zeus et vient vers les mortels pour les mener à l'assaut du ciel. Mais les hommes sont faibles, ou lâches; il faut les organiser. Ils aiment le plaisir et le bonheur immédiat; il faut leur apprendre à refuser, pour se grandir, le miel des jours. Ainsi, Prométhée, à son tour, devient un maître qui enseigne d'abord, commande ensuite. La lutte se prolonge encore et devient épuisante. Les hommes doutent d'aborder à la cité du soleil et si cette cité existe. Il faut les sauver d'eux-mêmes. Le héros leur dit alors qu'il connaît la cité, et qu'il est seul à la connaître. Ceux qui en doutent seront jetés au désert, cloués à un rocher, offerts en pâture aux oiseaux cruels. Les autres marcheront désormais dans les ténèbres, derrière le maître pensif et solitaire. Prométhée, seul, est devenu dieu et règne sur la solitude des hommes. Mais, de Zeus, il n'a conquis que la solitude et la cruauté; il n'est plus Prométhée, il est César. Le vrai, l'éternel Prométhée a pris maintenant le visage d'une de ses victimes. Le même cri, venu du fond des âges retentit toujours au fond du désert de Scythie. (*Essais*, p. 647.)

The modern rebel will thus defy the cult of reason as his two predecessors did faith. At the same time he knows that reason is the only evident means of ensuring the freedom and dignity of mankind. Camus thus sees modern man as torn by a seemingly irreconcilable dilemma of Sophoclean proportions:

> L'homme d'aujourd'hui qui crie sa révolte en sachant que cette révolte a des limites, qui exige la liberté et subit la nécessité, cet homme contradictoire, déchiré, désormais conscient de l'ambiguïté de l'homme et de son histoire, cet homme est l'homme tragique par excellence.

Camus's modern tragic hero, in short, is pitted not against feudal, Christian, right-wing society but against those who themselves defeated those forces in (predominantly eastern) Europe in the first half of this century. Prometheus has defected to the side of Zeus. Man must start all over again.

Camus's theory of modern tragedy, at least as far as *L'État de siège* and *Les Justes* are concerned, is irrevocably linked with his polemic against totalitarianism, particularly Stalinism, which dominated his work from 1945 onwards. *Les Justes* is crucial to this whole debate in so far as it is a very conscious effort at creating tragedy along classic lines and is at the same time set in the home of dialectical materialism during the time of transition. In order to understand the exact nature of the tragic dilemma which Camus wished to evoke in *Les Justes* it is necessary to examine in some detail the sources and genesis of the play. We shall then be in a position to come to certain conclusions about the well-known difficulty of reconciling history, tragedy and political commitment in general, and Camus's attempt to do so in particular.

One of the first references to *Les Justes* in the *Carnets* is to be found in an entry for the middle of June 1947, where the working title 'Kaliayev' is used. At this time Camus was preparing the sub-section of *L'Homme révolté* entitled 'Le Terrorisme individuel', and came across the historical figure of Kaliayev in Boris Savinkov's *Souvenirs d'un terroriste*, which had been translated into French in 1931. Camus saw in Kaliayev just what he needed for *L'Homme révolté*: a rebel with integrity, a man who, unlike the far better-known historical figures of Bakunin and Nechaev, refused to extend revolutionary action beyond certain limits, and who found a unique solution to the difficult ethical problem of tyrannicide. The very first reference to Kaliayev in the *Carnets* makes his significance for Camus quite clear:

Terrorisme.
   La grande pureté du terrorisme style Kaliayev, c'est que pour lui le meurtre coincide avec le suicide (cf. Savinkov: *Souvenirs d'un terroriste*). Une vie est payée par une vie. Le raisonnement

est faux, mais respectable. (Une vie ravie ne vaut pas une vie donnée.) Aujourd'hui le meurtre par procuration. Personne ne paye.

1905 Kaliayev: le sacrifice du corps. 1930: le sacrifice de l'esprit. (*Carnets* 2, p. 199.)

After this the play germinated rapidly in the autumn of 1947. The characters of Dora and Kaliayev ('Yanek') are clearly conceived from the outset and a long sketch for their love scene in Act 3 is in fact the first working note for the play. This is important. Kaliayev is to be championed in *L'Homme révolté* as the ideal rebel, who must essentially possess normal human emotions as a safeguard against the dehumanizing logic of Hegelian historicism. He must form a complete contrast with the terrifying robot visualized by Nechaev and Bakunin in the revolutionary catechism from which Camus quotes shortly afterwards in the *Carnets*:

Le révolutionnaire est un individu marqué. Il n'a ni intérêts ni affaires ni sentiments personnels, ni liens, rien qui lui soit propre, pas même de nom. Tout en lui est happé en vue d'un seul intérêt exclusif, d'une seule passion, la Révolution. (*Carnets* 2, p. 226.)

As is indicated by several entries at this time Camus was repelled by the inhuman extremism which characterized many of the anarcho-nihilists and bolshevists who, as he was to assert in *L'Homme révolté*, were the ancestors of the Stalinist tradition. Alternating with such entries are jottings for the play, for which no title yet exists, of the sort which show how Camus sought to emphasize the gulf between the ideal and the real terrorists of the day, and the consequent 'déchirement' which this caused for Kaliayev and Dora:

DORA. – Ce qu'il y a de triste, Yanek, c'est que tout cela nous vieillit. Plus jamais nous ne serons des enfants. Nous pouvons mourir désormais, nous avons fait le tour de l'homme. (Le meurtre, c'est la limite.)

– Non, Yanek, si la seule solution est la mort, alors nous ne sommes pas dans la bonne voie. La bonne voie est celle qui mène à la vie.

– Nous avons pris sur nous le malheur du monde, c'est un orgueil qui sera châtié.

– Nous sommes passés des amours enfantines à cette maîtresse première et dernière qui est la mort. Nous sommes allés trop vite. Nous ne sommes pas des hommes. (*Carnets* 2, p. 209.)

Roger Quilliot has suggested that with the relationship of Kaliayev and Dora Camus wished to 'réussir enfin une scène d'amour' and thus fill a gap in his work (*TRN*, p. 1815). But this was not how Camus worked: neither in the novel nor in the theatre was he a man for the 'scène à faire'. The love of Dora and Kaliayev is not so much an end in itself as a means. The evidence of the *Carnets* indicates that their intense and moving relationship served a fundamental philosophical purpose in the play, not primarily an artistic one. Camus sought to create revolutionaries who, although assassins, were as far removed as possible from the sort of revolutionary (Bakunin) who believed that 'la passion de la destruction est créatrice'. A line of dialogue jotted down for Dora points the contrast neatly: 'Si tu n'aimes rien, cela ne peut pas se terminer bien.'

Only two other characters are sketched at this early stage. 'Boris' will clearly develop into the leader of the group, Annenkov, modelled on Boris Savinkov himself. The other character has slightly more substance and is to be of far greater importance than Boris. He is referred to as 'le Tueur' and 'le réaliste' and is clearly the prototype of Stepan Fedorov:

LE T. – Dora est une femme et les femmes ne savent pas ce qu'est l'amour. . . . Cette terrible explosion où je vais m'anéantir c'est l'éclatement même de l'amour. (*Carnets* 2, p. 214.)

This is the only indication we have of his character, but already there is enough fanaticism and desperation in these few lines to suggest the whole of Stepan's role in *Les Justes*. Diametrically opposed to the moderate and human attitude of Kaliayev and Dora, it is he who provides the antithetical element in the 'affrontement de personnages égaux en force et en raison'.

From autumn 1947 onwards *Les Justes* and *L'Homme révolté* overlapped in their gestation. At the end of the year they merged completely in the publication of 'Les Meurtriers délicats' in the magazine *La Table Ronde*, in which Camus extolled the historical terrorists who were in the process of becoming the protagonists of his play. In 1903 the Revolutionary Socialist Party formed a terrorist group know as the Organisation de Combat under the leadership of Azef and then Savinkov. There then ensued a wave of assassinations constituting the second wave of terror, twenty years after the first which had resulted in the death of Alexander II in 1881. The pattern of assassinations this time was similar, many ministers and police and Government officials being accounted for by the bomb or revolver. Of royal personages the Grand Duke Sergei Alexandrovitch was the only victim, being blown up by a bomb thrown by Kaliayev in exactly the same circumstances as those which make up the plot of *Les Justes*. Camus is at pains throughout this article to stress the moral scrupulousness of the assassins. Kaliayev's failure to throw the bomb the first time was approved by the whole group, even though it placed them at great peril: 'à l'unanimité les terroristes décident qu'ils n'ont pas le droit de tuer des enfants.' This was consistent with their conduct generally. Savinkov vetoed a bomb attack on Admiral Dubasov in a train because it might endanger innocent passengers. At another time, when escaping from prison, he agreed with his comrade that if the necessity arose they would fire at the officers of the guard but shoot themselves rather than fire at ordinary guardsmen. The essential attraction of these terrorists for Camus, therefore, was that they had a strict sense of a limit beyond which they would not extend violence.

Once this is known it is possible to appreciate the importance of an original feature of *Les Justes* relative to the source material. Stepan Fedorov has no prototype in the *Souvenirs* and is quite foreign to the spirit of 'Les Meurtriers délicats'. Whereas Kaliayev, Dora, Annenkov and Voinov in the play were modelled on historical figures (Dora being Dora Brilliant and Voinov being Voinarovsky), Stepan was not – at least as far as the Organisation de Combat was concerned. It is significant that although Kaliayev, Dora and Annenkov were referred to in Camus's first notes by their Christian names, Stepan was impersonal to begin with, known only by the descriptive names 'le Tueur' and 'le réaliste'. He is a representative figure, standing for the ruthless Jacobin spirit of the extreme revolutionary according to tradition. He is a compound of earlier or contemporary figures such as Bakunin, Nechaev, Shigalev and Tkachev who came to believe that, in the words of Ivan Karamazov which Camus was fond of quoting: 'si Dieu n'existe pas, tout est permis' – one need not scruple to throw a bomb in the face of children. Dostoevsky's obsessive theme is central to *L'Homme révolté* and *Les Justes*, and is in fact echoed by Annenkov: 'Stepan . . . je ne puis te laisser dire que tout est permis.'

Camus's assassins are thus modelled on a small, isolated and exceptional group, 'les figures les plus extraordinaires du terrorisme russe', quite distinct from their terrorist ancestors and contemporaries in Russia, western Europe and the USA at this time. It is no doubt because of the invented character Stepan and all that he stands for that Camus asserted that although the plot of the play was basically authentic it nevertheless was not a historical play. Stepan is the means by which Camus throws the idealism of the group into relief. Without the idealist-realist dialectic Camus probably felt he could not fully achieve his didactic aim: 'J'ai seulement voulu montrer que l'action elle-même avait des limites. Il n'est de bonne et de juste action que celle qui reconnaît ces limites et qui, s'il lui faut les franchir, accepte au moins la mort.' It is arguable, however, that this didacticism, this moral and philosophical commitment on Camus's part, nevertheless prevented him from interpreting the assassination of the Grand

Duke with a degree of perspective sufficient to create an artistically coherent 'modern tragedy'. For despite Camus's assertion that *Les Justes* is not strictly speaking a historical play – thereby claiming for it the universality which tragedy must have – and despite also the impression it gives of being a preconceived debate fitted to a convenient historical event (rather in the manner of Anouilh's *Becket*, for example), the fact remains that *Les Justes* is nevertheless modelled on historical circumstances with a fidelity which is against all the traditions of French tragedy. It is true that Camus has created the absolutism-relativism debate by means of Stepan, and also generalized and conceptualized the crucial issue of redemptive suicide, which was only vaguely adumbrated in Savinkov. But apart from this Camus adheres as accurately as possible to the known facts of the assassination, particularly in the central dilemma over Kaliayev's refusal to kill the children. This fidelity to the facts vitiates the whole aspiration of the play to the status of tragedy in the following way.

A play which is based on the premiss that there is a limit beyond which human action must not pass can only be tragic to the extent that it portrays a protagonist who, perhaps through some form of *hubris* (but not essentially), loses sufficient control of himself to move from *mesure* to *démesure*. In *Les Justes* there is some confusion as to what constitutes the limit separating the two concepts. That is to say, in the terms of Camus's political philosophy, what is the point at which justifiable and reasonably ethical revolutionary activity becomes unjustifiable, brutal terrorism, aiming at quick results, ostensibly because of sympathy for the oppressed, but in truth, according to Camus, motivated by hatred of the oppressor and little more? Is it murder, or is it only certain kinds of murder? In *Les Justes* there are two limits: the first, which is intensely personal to the author, is the total sanctity of life. Camus's early note for the play suggests that *all* murder constituted the limit: 'le meurtre, c'est la limite'. In that case the assassins have to all intents and purposes already gone beyond this limit at the outset of the play by having firmly resolved to assassinate the Grand Duke. It is clear from the importance which Camus attached to the theme of redemptive suicide that the tragic action in the play is the assassination itself, which is only the consummation of the movement of tragic involvement which began for Kaliayev, Dora and the others the day they compromised the purity of their ideals by finally resorting to terrorism: 'Il n'est de bonne et de juste action que celle qui reconnaît ces limites et qui, s'il lui faut les franchir, accepte au moins la mort.' Quilliot has understood best the extent to which all of the assassins were tragic, condemned figures throughout the play:

L'air que respirent les Justes a la légèreté écrasante des altitudes alpestres. En dépit de leur ardeur, il fait froid parmi eux. Tout le dernier acte, en pleine floraison printanière, est scandé par les plaintes de Dora: 'J'ai froid.' Les Justes vivent un éternel hiver . . . Les yeux de Dora sont tristes, Kaliayev est triste, de cette tristesse lancinante des cauchemars. Chacun porte sur son front comme le sacre de la mort. Et cela nous les rend par instants aussi étranges que Lazare le ressuscité. A force de tendre toutes leurs énergies au service d'une passion, les Justes se sont séparés du monde vivant.[1]

As is shown most acutely in Kaliayev and Dora, they are living in a hell on earth, that irrevocable state of damnation which was for Dostoevsky 'the suffering of being unable to love'. They are living their punishment in advance of their crime. In this context of a tragedy of suffering, of a conflict *within* the terrorists between the rival calls of life and love on the one hand and justice on the other, it is ultimately Dora who is the most tragic figure. Kaliayev dies with his ideals intact. He is sublime, heroic, epic, not tragic. Dora, on the other hand, at the end of Act 5 attains a tragic stature when, unlike Kaliayev, she hardens herself and brings herself to 'resemble Stepan'. Having lost her love, she literally renounces her femininity and her humanity for the sake of justice: 'Tout sera plus facile maintenant.' The weakness of the play is that this interesting tragic perspective is presented literally at the final curtain, exactly like the one which opens up on Maria at the end of *Le Malentendu* after the audience's reservoir of tragic empathy has been exhausted during the course of the play. And in the theatre too the play as tragedy at this level will have been compromised for those who do not grasp Camus's premiss – that the characters, having arrogated to themselves the power of life and death in any circumstances whatsoever, have already fallen into a metaphysical limbo long before the action of the play begins. The point is all the more easily lost in the theatre for any spectator who is not a total pacifist, since the assassination of a supposed tyrant does not automatically provoke revulsion and metaphysical anguish.

The real limit in the play at the obvious dramatic level is the killing of *children*, which is an extension and refinement of the first, the sanctity of *all* life. Camus has now moved from the absolute position of a Tarrou (all execution is wrong) to a relative position (most, but not all, executions are wrong) which turns *Les Justes* into an ostensibly more accessible political play about the ends versus the means. Now the assassination of the Grand Duke is of secondary importance. From the moment in the second act when Kaliayev fails to throw the bomb the debate is not so much: can one kill in the interests of the revolution? as, since one *can* kill in the interests of the revolution (by paying with one's life), *can one also kill children* if absolutely necessary? The initial limit appears to be forgotten:

> DORA. Yanek accepte de tuer le grand-duc puisque sa mort peut avancer le temps où les enfants russes ne mourront plus de faim. Cela déjà n'est pas facile. Mais la mort des neveux du grand-duc n'empêchera aucun enfant de mourir de faim. Même dans la destruction, il y a un ordre, il y a des limites.
> STEPAN (*violemment*). Il n'y a pas de limites . . . (*TRN*, pp. 337–8.)

Dora here stresses the pointlessness of killing children, and elsewhere the great tactical harm it would do their movement, since this is the best way of reasoning with Stepan. But by her 'il y a des limites' she is really expressing the moral repugnance she shares with all the others except Stepan for such action. Once one accepts that the real issue is that of *mesure* and *démesure* the play loses its tragic appeal. For having to assassinate a man who is a leading representative of an inhuman and despotic system, *and succeeding in doing it without exceeding a crucial ethical limit* (the distinction between a culpable adult and an innocent child), makes Kaliayev not a tragic figure in any dramatic sense but rather the exemplary hero of a didactic melodrama exactly as defined by Camus in Athens. Not only exemplary but lucky, since fate sees to it, just as in the historical circumstances, that he is not faced a second time with the dilemma of deciding whether or not to kill the children. One feels that Anouilh or Sartre, each for different reasons, would not have allowed Kaliayev to slip off the hook so easily.

Out of respect for the essential facts of the historical incident, Camus has not weighted circumstances heavily enough against Kaliayev for his ideals – his sense of limits – to be strained to breaking-point. Kaliayev is allowed to be what Camus obviously believed him to be in real life: the ideal rebel, a prototype of the perfect anti-Stalinist. He is too humble, too scrupulous, too flawless to be tragic in the accepted dramatic sense. He has no *hamartia* and consequently no anagnorisis, and what is tragedy without them? Although Camus claimed to have created a classical conflict – 'l'affrontement de personnages égaux en force et en raison' – he has not succeeded. Kaliayev is obviously right, Stepan only too palpably wrong. In modifying the historical context by creating the character of Stepan, he failed to exploit the political and ethical contrast with Kaliayev in full theatrical terms. He lacked the emotional detachment with which Sartre constructed a similar conflict between Hugo and Hoederer in *Les Mains sales*; that same detachment and craftsmanship with which Anouilh in *Antigone* brings his audience round against all the odds to see that perhaps Creon has a point after all: 'il faut pourtant qu'il y en ait qui disent oui.' Camus is in fact trying to do three things at once in *Les Justes*: first, create a tragedy in accordance with a number of basic aesthetic principles, secondly, make a committed statement about a twentieth-century disease of the political mind, and finally do honour to the memory of a group of exemplary historical figures exactly as they lived and died in the documented circumstances of 1905. The fact that Camus stressed that he was not writing a historical play evidently did not mean that he was prepared to alter the details of the assassination sufficiently to make Kaliayev a tragic hero in a truly classic and dramatic sense.

The fundamental weakness of *Les Justes* as an attempt at modern tragedy is that there are two structural antagonisms, both potentially tragic but, as handled by Camus, pulling against each other and dissipating the tension. First there is the play about 1905: Kaliayev and friends versus the established forces of Tsarist Russia. In Hebbel's terms, an individual representing a new order challenges the old order: he is crushed but not without making his mark. Nine playwrights out of ten, basing an attempt at modern tragedy on the assassination of the Grand Duke Sergei in 1905, would have structured their play on this conflict. Camus, however, is the one playwright in ten who, anachronistically, saw this historical event as the occasion for a veiled statement about Stalinism and political expediency in general. He thus created a rival antagonism: Kaliayev the Idealist, the Creator, the Poet (cf. Greek 'poieein', to make) versus Stepan the Realist, the Destroyer, the Killer, the archetypal Stalinist. As Kaliayev tells him, 'derrière ce que tu dis, je vois s'annoncer un despotisme qui, s'il s'installe jamais, fera de moi un assassin alors que j'essaie d'être un justicier.' Dora makes the same point: 'D'autres viendront peut-être qui s'autoriseront de nous pour tuer et qui ne paieront pas de leur vie.' But this back-dated vision of Stalinism is not the order of the day; it is not the force which crushes Kaliayev. In strict dramatic terms it is an intrusion, a propaganda digression revealing the extent to which Camus's political and moral obsessions of 1946–8 impaired his artistic judgement. The pretensions of *Les Justes* to modern tragedy, then, are vitiated by the fact that the play contains two parallel, antithetical structures which overlap but never coincide: Kaliayev versus Tsarism, and Kaliayev versus ur-Stalinism. The first is tragic (in a loose, popular sense, in so far as the assassination of the Grand Duke, like all execution, is physically and spiritually degrading) but not dramatic, the second dramatic but not tragic. The two could have coincided only if Camus had had sufficient courage to discard the strict historical framework of the assassination after the failure of the first attempt. Just briefly in Act 2 there is a suggestion of the way in which Camus's dramatic instinct might have led him:

> KALIAYEV. Regardez-moi, frères, regarde-moi, Boria, je ne suis pas un lâche, je n'ai pas reculé. Je ne les attendais pas. Tout s'est passé trop vite. Ces deux petits visages sérieux et dans ma main, ce poids terrible. C'est sur eux qu'il fallait le lancer. Ainsi. Tout droit. Oh, non! Je n'ai pas pu. (*Il tourne son regard de l'un à l'autre.*)

One wonders if the Anouilh of *Antigone*, the Sartre of *Les Mains sales* or the Beauvoir of *Les Bouches inutiles* would have failed to recognize the tragic potential of this vision? Would their artistic instinct have allowed them to leave the children out of the coach the second time? Tragedy is precisely about men in impossible circumstances, being driven by external pressures – the insinuations of an Iago or, say, the taunts of a Stepan Fedorov – to commit actions which in normal circumstances would be unthinkable, so horrifying that after the failure of the first attempt they close their eyes like Kaliayev and say 'Oh, non! Je n'ai pas pu.' In terms of dramatic action *Les Justes* is scarcely more tragic than the *Oresteia* would have been if Orestes had drawn the line after exacting his just vengeance on Aegisthus and decided to spare Clytemnestra. For Aeschylus it was evil to kill one's mother. But in certain circumstances – such as at the command of Apollo – it was inevitable, and tragic. For Camus it is evil to kill children. In no circumstances is it inevitable. And so children are not killed. Camus would not have their blood on Kaliayev's hands any more than Nahum Tate in the eighteenth century would have

Lear's aberration culminate in the death of Cordelia. Thus for three acts Camus points his play in the right direction for a genuinely dramatic and tragic consummation, builds up to a potentially tragic climax – and then commits what can best be compared to coitus interruptus. The last two acts are an anticlimax in every way. At the end of the play Kaliayev inspires in us a warm glow, which may have much to do with moral approbation but which has none of that combination of pity, terror and aesthetic pleasure that comes from watching an ineluctable tragic movement work itself out.

It is tempting to talk of a failure of the imagination on Camus's part, but it is in fact all too easy to misunderstand his purpose in *Les Justes*. If he did not contemplate for one minute making any radical alteration to the facts of the 1905 assassination, it was because the plot he dug out of Savinkov was already richly suggestive for his all-important anti-totalitarian polemics of the years immediately following 1945 – and that was enough for him. Ironically, it is conceivable that if Camus had backed up his claim that he was not writing a historical play with greater conviction, and brought Kaliayev, under pressure, to commit the atrocity I have proposed – which would in fact have made it a much more Sartrian sort of play – he might, by implication, have made his point about Stalinism with greater effect, and at the same time achieved that synthesis of drama, tragedy and ethics which eluded him after *Caligula*.

7 Stalemate: Translations and Adaptations

C'est du moins là un vice que je peux satisfaire sans m'offrir à la réprobation.

Camus

Quand même on pense au bernard l'hermite, qui cuirasse d'une coquille massive, empruntée à une autre espèce animale, les côtés vulnérables de sa nature; ou encore aux martiens de Wells, minuscules et chétifs au sommet de leurs tripodes invincibles.

Robert Poulet

Many found it surprising that after the success of *Les Justes* Camus produced no more completely original work for the theatre. During the last ten years of his life he contented himself with translating or adapting six works by other authors. They were, with their French titles and year of performance in Paris (or Angers, where stated):

1953　*Les Esprits* – Pierre de Larivey
1953　*La Dévotion à la croix* – Calderón
　　　　(both directed by Marcel Herrand at the Festival d'Art Dramatique d'Angers in June)
1955　*Un Cas intéressant* – Dino Buzzati
1956　*Requiem pour une nonne* – Faulkner
1957　*Le Chevalier d'Olmedo* – Lope de Vega
　　　　(Angers Festival)
1959　*Les Possédés* – Dostoevsky

The whole of the last decade of Camus's life was a period of meagre production in all media: after the publication of *L'Homme révolté* in November 1951 only the novel *La Chute* and the six

119

short stories in *L'Exil et le royaume*. Camus's detractors, particularly the Communists and the Left in general, considererd he was burnt out: *L'Homme révolté* was his last will and testament as far as they were concerned. He had sold out to the bourgeoisie, and what further proof was needed than the fact that when the Algerian rebellion erupted in late 1954 Camus refused to side automatically with the Algerian nationalists? Camus was particularly depressed by the polemics of the magazine *Les Temps modernes*, the quarrel with Francis Jeanson and Jean-Paul Sartre and the eventual break with the latter. With regard to his theatrical activities in the 1950s one of the most virulent critics was Robert Poulet who likened Camus to a hermit crab taking refuge inside the massive genius of artists such as Calderón and Dostoevsky. In Poulet's eyes not only was Camus sterile and parasitic; his choice of authors was proof that he was a right-wing reactionary. Instancing Calderón, Faulkner and Dostoevsky, he accused Camus of having allied himself intellectually and spiritually with 'successivement, le défenseur espagnol de la monarchie théocratique, le représentant américain du patriciat sudiste, le contempteur russe de l'anarchie et de la démocratie'.[1] Although this particular diatribe was not delivered until 1959 its tone is not untypical of the sort of attack Camus had to face from 1952 onwards.

In these circumstances it is understandable that Camus's work as a translator and adaptor served as a form of therapy, an escape from the hypercritical world of Paris intellectuals. He frequently stated that the theatre was, with the soccer field, one of the few places in the world where he felt completely at ease. At the same time he needed to escape not only from detractors but from the countless claims on his time which resulted from his national eminence: requests for him to sign petitions and manifestos, give interviews, produce articles and lectures out of a hat, and, as he himself put it somewhat facetiously, generally do something on behalf of the orphans of Kashmir and the lepers of New Hebrides.

It is not strictly true that Camus wrote nothing original whatsoever for the theatre after *Les Justes*: he did in fact write a short mime-play *La Vie d'artiste*, which was published in *Simoun* in 1953 but does not so far appear to have been performed. It is closely linked to 'Jonas ou l'Artiste au travail', the most ironic and absurd of the six stories in *L'Exil et le royaume*, which examines the predicament (Camus's own) of the artist in contemporary society. Popularity means financial security but at the same time may dissipate the artist's energy and inspiration. Obscurity on the other hand leaves the artist sufficiently free from social chores to devote himself to his art, yet results in physical and emotional suffering for himself and his family. The artist cannot create in isolation from society, since he is bonded to it materially and psychologically. Both the story and the mime-play are about the difficulty if not impossibility for the artist to be both *solitaire* and *solidaire*, detached enough from society to possess the time and objectivity to create, and yet at the same time sufficiently part of it to gain the necessary spiritual and material sustenance. It is a vicious circle of which almost all artists and writers in modern times are in some measure a victim.

Four of the six stories in *L'Exil et le royaume* are set in Algeria, and Quilliot has called the book appropriately 'un pèlerinage aux sources', a spiritual return by Camus to his first inspiration. His work in the theatre at this time is partly the same sort of experience, since in translating and adapting plays and then collaborating in the productions Camus was reliving the happiness he had known in the Théâtre du Travail and the Théâtre de l'Équipe between 1935 and 1939. It is customary to discount the importance of this period of Camus's theatrical activity. To a certain extent it is true that some of these translations and adaptations are nothing more than 'a kind of diversion or distraction from his other creative activities' (Couch).[2] Yet others, notably *Les Possédés* and *Requiem pour une nonne*, are very revealing about Camus's dramatic craftsmanship – and limitations – as well as being of some importance for a study of his ideas.

The first of the six plays provides an immediate link with Camus's Algerian apprenticeship. Pierre de Larivey's *Les Esprits* was first adapted by Camus in 1940 with the Équipe in mind. It was first performed by a student company in Algiers in 1946, but the version produced for the Angers Festival in 1953 was completely revised. Larivey's play, dating from the 1570s, is a gay but slight comedy, in its style transitional between the Italian *commedia erudita* and French classical comedy. Larivey helped himself liberally to slices of Terence, Plautus and Lorenzino dei Medici, before being cannibalized in turn by Molière: *Les Esprits* is in fact one of the links between Plautus' *Aulularia* and Molière's *L'Avare*. As it stands it has many features which would militate against a successful modern production of a Renaissance play: obscure and archaic language, an unnecessary sub-plot, and in general a gratuitous and poorly controlled intrigue, containing, as Camus admitted, 'des longueurs insupportables'. Camus shortened the play from five to three acts, eliminated three characters (Elisabeth, Pasquette and Désiré), cut much of the dialogue and modernized the rest.

The basic plot remains the same. Two young men, Fortuné and Urbain, conspire to marry the women of their choice, having first bedded them with the mirthful abandon of pre-classical comedy. Urbain's father is a miser and is forced to consent to his son's marriage by being made to believe that his hoard has been stolen and that his house is haunted by ghosts (*les esprits*). The agent of victory is Fortuné's wily valet, Frontin, for whom Camus prescribed in his notes in 1940 'le costume d'Arlequin'. He has edited and streamlined the play skilfully, but even so it remains bitty and insubstantial – curiously, containing not a single female speaking-part. The intrigue of *Les Esprits* is still very loosely jointed by classical standards. For example, Urbain is not faced with any rival claimant for Féliciane's hand, and Fortuné is in fact *aided* in his suit by his benign father. Social and parental pressures of the sort which Molière inflicted on his thwarted couples are lacking, and indeed the complicated social fabric of middle-class respectability which is intricately bound up with Molière's plots has no counterpart in Larivey's play. For example, Fortuné's beloved is nine months pregnant, and the abbess into whose convent she was due to go cheerfully settles for fifty per cent of the girl's inheritance instead.

Camus's interest in the play was to a large extent technical. In its characterization it suggests some of the elements of the *commedia dell'arte* (in so far as any play can which is completely dialogued). A detailed letter of 1940 prescribed this sort of production, regardless of whether it was strictly appropriate to the genre (*TRN*, pp. 1847–8). The play was thus originally a pretext, the raw material for *travaux pratiques* during Camus's apprenticeship with the Équipe. It afforded him the technical challenge of simulating the *commedia dell'arte*, and is further proof of the complete break which the Équipe made with the Théâtre du Travail. The 1953 text of the play makes allowance for stylized masks and costumes, mimes and acrobatics. Camus even takes the (for him) unique step of describing in a footnote *à la Feydeau* the way in which an effect is to be obtained, a small detail perhaps but nevertheless revealing the extent to which purely material considerations appealed to his imagination in this adaptation:

> Deux rues séparent les trois maisons. Les personnages rentrent et sortent de chez eux, font mille tours et se livrent à des chassés-croisés. A la cour et au jardin, ils entrent en bondissant sur des tremplins dissimulés en coulisse. (*TRN*, p. 445.)

This *comédie à l'italienne* was not Camus's only contact with the Italian theatre in this period. In 1955 he adapted Dino Buzzati's *Un Caso Clinico* under the French title *Un Cas intéressant* at the request of Georges Vitaly and Ludmila Vlasto. The play had a reasonably successful run in the same year, opening on 12 March at the Théâtre La Bruyère. The play is at the exact theatrical extreme from *Les Esprits* and is much nearer to the absurd universe of the French theatre of the 1950s and 1960s. It is a tragi-comic study – Buzzati in fact speaks of 'ma comédie' – of gradual demoralization and death in hallucinatory circumstances. And yet just as Camus appreciated *Les Esprits* as a vehicle for a somewhat spurious *commedia dell'arte* vitality and spontaneity, so once again he looked to Italian theatre as an embodiment of what he most admired in European civilization. In an essay of 1937 on Mediterranean civilization Camus had stressed his belief that Italian Fascism was very different – less inhuman, totalitarian – from German National Socialism at that time (*Essais*, pp. 1321–7). In Italy ideology had to bend to accommodate the country and the people, and not vice versa as was the case in northern Europe. Now almost twenty years later, in the preface to *Un Cas intéressant*, Camus was to say the same thing in different terms about the darker philosophical aspect of Buzzati's work (Camus had already read his *Il Deserto dei Tartari* before being asked to adapt *Un Caso Clinico*):

> Dans tout ce que font aujourd'hui nos amis italiens, il y a une générosité, une chaleur du cœur, une simplicité vivante qui manque un peu dans nos œuvres françaises . . . Même lorsque les Italiens passent par la porte étroite que leur montrent Kafka ou Dostoievski, ils y passent avec tout leur poids de chair. Et leur noirceur rayonne encore . . . (*TRN*, p. 599.)

Working with a French translation of the Italian play Camus produced a French stage version in a mere fifteen days. It is not difficult to imagine Camus working with such relative speed on a text presenting a world with which he was already so familiar. In his preface Camus mentioned the similarity of the work to Tolstoy's *Death of Ivan Ilyitch*. A no less appropriate comparison might be made with *Le Malentendu*. A prosperous and seemingly healthy and happy family man, Giovanni Corte, moves inexorably to his death. His family seem to be accomplices; when his mother finally tries to rescue him from the clinic where he is being treated against his wishes it is too late, just as Jan's mother comes too late to prevent him from drinking the drugged tea. The striking similarity between the two works is further reinforced by the presence in *Un Cas intéressant* of a silent and sinister woman who makes one or two entrances during the play for no reason: they are just as unaccountable on a literal level as those of 'le Vieux'. She is a sort of banshee, and whenever she appears Corte hears a wailing noise. Corte dies in the last scene and the nurse attending him turns out to be the banshee once again. Giovanni Corte, like Jan, is an isolated individual in a world which, despite, and in some cases because of, friends, relatives, wealth and security, is hostile and absurd.

Though sharing the same theme, the two plays differ in style and structure. *Le Malentendu* is an original play in a rather conventional genre, stretching dialogue and symbol to the limits of that genre. Buzzati's play on the other hand is clearly on this side of the 1950 dividing line. Many absurdist plays are carefully controlled exercises in gradation, or perhaps one might say – since some of this literature is a metaphor of the political and military nightmares of the twentieth century – in *escalation*. These dramatists ask the same question as Sartre and Camus: where does one draw the line? or, to use Camus's terms, what is the *limit* to the horror one can commit or allow to be committed? But *L'État de siège*, *Les Justes*, *Les Mains sales*, *Les Mouches* are cast in the traditional form of highly articulate debates, *agons* with a pro-con dialectic. The absurdist dramatists have tried to perfect a form which affects the spectator on a much more psychic and less intellectual level. The form and structure are a metaphor of the feeling of creeping powerlessness that contemporary man experiences as he is dehumanized by a slow but steady proliferation of material objects, an intensification and escalation of propaganda, or, as in the striking example provided by Buzzati's play, by a degradation of his personal status. Now there are no more heroes and villains ranged on opposite sides of a nineteenth-century dialectic, just ordinary men like Béranger, Biedermann, Professor Taranne, Corte and Jan submerged by a rising tide of irrationality and violence. Corte is degraded literally and figuratively by being moved down the successive floors of the clinic, which, like many another clinic, sanatorium, mental home or prison in modern literature, is a symbol of society as a whole. He is told that from the sixth floor downwards the clinic accommodates increasingly serious cases, but in *his* case there is nothing to worry about – his descent each time is only temporary. He is finally persuaded to move to the ground floor, death, having lost his will to survive, to protest, to insist on being moved upwards for a change.

Just as the structure of the play is based on degradation, so the dialogue on occasion brilliantly and horrifically conveys the effect of articulate language, that of professional men, the language burlesqued by Beckett's Lucky in *Waiting for Godot*, being used, misused, debased, degraded, to talk a man into the grave. It is here that Buzzati has been admirably served by having Camus, the ironist of *La Peste*, 'Jonas', *La Chute* and the second half of *L'Étranger*, to rework the French version of the play. In its form, then, *Un Cas intéressant* is very characteristic of the *avant-garde* theatre of the 1950s and 1960s. Step by step the fire-raisers take control of Biedermann's house and stock it, increasingly obviously, with inflammable material; the body in *Amédée ou Comment s'en débarrasser* grows; Ionesco's Fascist rhinoceroses increase in number. At least one work by Camus in the 1950s, 'Jonas' (and of course the mime-play based on it), has precisely this characteristic absurdist structure. It may be recalled, finally, that it was not until the 1958 version of *Le Malentendu* that Camus removed 'le Vieux' from the plane of naturalism and attempted to make him more of a symbol of the absurd. Before this last version the final curtain 'Non!' was unprepared: there was no build-up (or escalation). It is not altogether unreasonable, in conclusion, to speculate that it was the influence of *Un Cas intéressant* and plays like it in the 1950s which, admittedly in a minor way, gave Camus this artistic insight into one of the formal difficulties of *Le Malentendu*.

Even more than Camus admired Italian civilization, he understood and respected Spain and the Spanish people. His mother was of Spanish descent as were a large percentage of the *pieds noirs* with whom he grew up in Algiers. What he claimed as distinctive and admirable in the Spanish character was personal pride, a punctilious sense of honour and a frank enjoyment of pleasure: 'Il y a une certaine aisance dans la joie qui définit la vraie civilisation. Et le peuple espagnol est un des rares en Europe qui soit civilisé.' (*Essais*, p. 41.) These characteristics have a prominent place in Camus's writing at all times, notably as idealized features of his composite Mediterranean man. In addition, the Spanish theatre of the Golden Age vied with the classical Greek and the Shakespearean as his favourite type of theatre. Passion, heroism, tenderness, honour, mystery, these were what Camus welcomed as a change from the drab conventions of naturalism and indeed as a change from life itself in the twentieth century: 'Dans notre Europe des cendres, Lope de Vega et le théâtre espagnol peuvent apporter aujourd'hui leur inépuisable lumière, leur insolite jeunesse, nous aider à retrouver sur nos scènes l'esprit de grandeur pour servir enfin l'avenir véritable de notre théâtre.' (*TRN*, p. 176.)

Spain figures prominently in Camus's theatrical activities before the 1950s; first as the setting for *L'État de siège* and *Révolte dans les Asturies*, secondly we may remember that Fernando da Rojas's *La Celestina* was one of the productions of L'Équipe, and Cervantes's *Comédie des Bagnes d'Algers* was scheduled for production when the war broke out. It is by no means surprising, then, to find two Golden Age dramas amongst Camus's translations of this period: Calderón's *La Devoción de la Cruz* (*La Dévotion à la croix*) which was put on at the same time as *Les Esprits* at the 1953 Angers Festival, and Lope de Vega's *El Cabellero de Olmedo* (*Le Chevalier d'Olmedo*) four years later at the same festival and directed by Camus himself. Since both plays are in fact straight translations with no modifications to the text, they present perhaps less interest for a study of Camus's theory and practice in the theatre than the other plays with which he was associated during this period. Opinions vary about the quality of the translations, however. His rendering of *La Devoción de la Cruz* has been attacked by Ricardo Paseyro with a passion bordering on lust.[3] Although many of the 'bévues' gleefully listed by Paseyro are really only inaccuracies necessitated by the rhythm of workable dialogue in French, he nevertheless has a point when he suggests that Camus has misinterpreted Calderón's message in the play. Calderón, a Molinist, intended *La Devoción de la Cruz* to be a resounding affirmation of the Spanish Jesuit's doctrine reconciling predestination and free will. Grace is granted only to the *Elect*; free will, on the other hand, is enjoyed by all men. However, grace is confirmed on the Elect only if they have made good use of their free will. Paseyro maintains that Camus appears to consider Calderón a Thomist, and indeed it is plain in the preface that Camus has missed the subtlety of the compromise contributed to the Counter-Reformation by Molina. If the play were, as Camus asserts, an illustration of the doctrine that 'tout est grâce' the whole point would be lost. The devotion which Eusebio vows to the cross of Christ is the expression of his free will. It is this devotion alone, because faithfully observed, which brings about confirmation of his grace at the end of the play. Eusebio's original election may have been arbitrary and predestined, but its confirmation was not. Calderón, in this play at least, is the most faithful of Molinists, and he does not allow his message to escape his audience. Paseyro maintains that on a number of occasions Camus makes Eusebio more dependent on 'la force souveraine' than any Jesuit author – even a Molinist – could have done. Nevertheless it may be said in Camus's defence that in general terms the Molinist doctrine would have been clear enough to anyone who went specifically to Angers in 1953 to hear it. The *libertad* which Eusebio and Julia proclaim at various points in the play is translated correctly enough, as are speeches by Alberto and Curcio which stress that Eusebio has *deserved* the grace which is accorded him in the last scene.

For his adaptations of Calderón and Lope Camus made use of existing translations and the advice of friends whose Spanish was better than his own. He subscribed to the modern view that a dramatist, aided if necessary by a translator-informant, can produce a more stageworthy text than the average professional translator who, while being more faithful to the original, is probably less capable of phrasing actable dialogue. This was Camus's concern in both these enterprises, and in his programme notes to *Le Chevalier d'Olmedo* he put a good case:

N'importe quel acteur sait qu'il est difficile de dire une réplique qui commence par un participe présent ou par une subordonnée,

Une telle phrase, courante dans les traductions dont nous disposons, manque de ce qu'on appelle au théâtre 'l'attaque'. Une proposition principale, le verbe actif, le cri, la dénégation, l'interrogation, le vocatif sont au contraire les éléments d'un texte en action, qui exprime directement le personnage en même temps qu'il entraîne l'acteur. (*TRN*, p. 715.)

Camus's prose versions of both these plays work reasonably well, given the difficulty of capturing the baroque exuberance of the Spanish texts, particularly the Lope de Vega with its wide range of tonal and stylistic elements: amatory lyricism, burlesque, heroic tirade, familiar harangue and comic *quiproquo*. Lope in fact offered Camus much more of a challenge, both linguistically and theatrically, than Calderón. He is a less ostentatiously religious and philosophical dramatist than Calderón, and more 'Shakespearean', possessing a much more instinctive mastery of dramatic effects, changing moods, and a richer, more varied style of dialogue. With its romantic theme, the love of a perfect knight, Don Alonso, for Doña Ines, and the murder of Don Alonso by a cowardly rival, *Le Chevalier d'Olmedo* epitomizes the sort of Golden Age play admired by Camus. The attractions for him of plays such as these are obvious. They are completely consistent with his preference, expressed in the manifesto of the Équipe twenty years earlier, for 'la vérité et la simplicité, la violence dans les sentiments et la cruauté dans l'action. Ainsi se tournera-t-il [le Théâtre de l'Équipe] vers les époques où l'amour de la vie se mêlait au désespoir de vivre.' (*TRN*, p. 1690.)

In his frequent linking of the Spanish and Elizabethan theatres Camus, taking 'Elizabethan' to include the Jacobean theatre, sought as his common denominator what Robert Pignarre in his definition of 'l'éthique élisabéthaine' calls 'l'ivresse de vivre':

Sous la menace puritaine, ce théâtre fait éclater le chant du paganisme renaissant. Il clame éperdument l'ivresse de vivre sans autre règle que de demeurer fidèle à l'essence de son être. Tout en poursuivant la pureté à travers le paroxysme, et bien qu'ils dédaignent toute censure, ses héros restent soumis aux impulsions élémentaires. .... Dans le sang, dans le crime, dans la folie, dans la cruauté, dans la vengeance et jusque dans l'inceste et l'homosexualité, ils peuvent se proclamer, comme le Félice de Marston, 'parfaitement d'accord avec le bonheur universel'. Leur individualisme trop tendu finit par se résoudre en frénésie panique. Nulle part la tragédie n'a célébré avec une ivresse plus superbe la puissance de la vie s'affirmant dans la souffrance et la destruction.[4]

Le Chevalier d'Olmedo and *La Dévotion à la croix* thus follow on quite naturally from Camus's earlier productions of *La Celestina*, *The Silent Woman* and the projected production of *Othello*. These productions of the thirties were in turn well within the mainstream of fashion started at the beginning of the century by Antoine's and Lugné-Poe's productions of Shakespeare, and Copeau's *A Woman Killed with Kindness* (Heywood) in 1913. Such theatre can be seen to be completely consistent with the anticommercial aims of the *avant-garde*. Much of it is suitable for open-air production, and this helps to break the bourgeois Parisian stranglehold on the French theatre by creating new audiences, both regionally and socially. The biggest break of all is with the drab, pseudo-realistic language, décor and stage conventions of naturalism. The Renaissance theatre of Spain and England gripped Camus's imagination as much as it did Copeau's, and for roughly the same reasons. It was a return to a much more metaphysical and ritual concept of theatre, far closer to the roots of human existence than most European theatre since the end of the seventeenth century. At the same time it made the greatest possible demands on the imagination of the director and rehabilitated the full range of theatre arts, many of which – mime, music, symbolic décor, stylized costume – had virtually vanished during the nineteenth century, or had ceased to be practised with consistency and sensitivity.

With his adaptation of William Faulkner's *Requiem for a Nun* Camus enjoyed a success in the Parisian theatre which far exceeded that of his two best original plays, *Caligula* and *Les Justes*. Although the task of adapting the novel fell to Camus by chance – the death of his actor friend, Marcel Herrand, who was due to do it – Camus had been familiar with and had admired Faulkner's work since before the war. 'Le plus grand romancier américain', 'le plus grand romancier contemporain', as Camus considered him, was, with his fellow 'Southerner' Caldwell, listed in the prospective repertory of the Équipe in 1936 along with dramatists who represented 'la violence dans les sentiments et la cruauté dans l'action'. There is no short measure of these characteristics in *Requiem for a Nun* or the novel to which it is a sequel, *Sanctuary*. Steeped in depravity, infanticide, humiliation and suffering, Faulkner's work was considered by Camus to possess a very great dramatic intensity, sufficient in fact to come close to realizing his own ideal of modern tragedy: 'Faulkner laisse entrevoir le temps où le tragique de notre histoire pourra enfin porter cothurne.' (*TRN*, p. 1871.)

Requiem for a Nun possesses a unique advantage for stage adaptation. It is highly original in that all its action is presented in dialogue form. This dramatic text of the novel is divided into three acts which are in turn divided into scenes. Every act or scene is set by the author by means of detailed directions, and he also observes the conventions of the playwright with regard to lighting, movements of actors, and timing of the curtain. Indeed Faulkner demonstrates in places a very shrewd awareness of the playwright's craft. Some of the most powerful moments in Camus's stage version, the short opening scene, the flashback to the murder of the child, and Temple's 'confession' in the Governor's office without knowing of her husband's presence, are lifted straight from the novel with only the slightest refinement of detail on Camus's part. What distinguishes the novel nevertheless from a conventional dramatic script is the fact that each act is prefaced by a lyrical description and historical account of the building which it is set in or associated with. They are the courthouse, the Golden Dome (the Governor's residence) and the jail, and represent for Faulkner the different stages of the implacable justice exacted by man. In the religious context implicit in the title of the work, these institutions symbolize, respectively, in Camus's own words: 'un temple . . . un confessionnal . . . et un couvent où la négresse vouée à la mort rachète son crime et celui de Temple Stevens.' (*TRN*, p. 1858.) In purely dramatic terms these sections, which together make up one-third of the whole work, are as textually independent of, and detachable from, the 'script' as, say, Shaw's prefaces to his plays. Something of the atmosphere which Faulkner wished to create for the work is lost, as Camus admitted, but the fact nevertheless remains that the whole of the dramatized sections of the novel are just about viable as they stand.

Working with M. E. Coindreau's French translation of the novel, Camus produced a French stage version which keeps very close to Faulkner's scenario and dialogue. Inevitably he found it necessary to make a small number of modifications of the sort which are necessitated by the demands of the stage. He reshaped one or two incidents to intensify their impact in the theatre. The opening scene is a good example. In Faulkner's text Nancy is briefly sentenced to death, to which she replies, 'Yes, Lord.' The enormity of this act of contempt of court in the eyes of Faulkner's Southern whites and the ensuing uproar are suggested by his stage directions, which include the effect: 'The curtain starts hurriedly and jerkily down as if the judge, officers, the court itself were jerking frantically at it to hide this disgraceful business . . .' This is contained word for word in the Camus version, but the impact on the audience is intensified by the fact that the judge, and Nancy's advocate, Gavin Stevens, have each been given a long speech by Camus in which they have solemnly warned her that she must not speak once the sentence has been pronounced. They also refer to the earlier irregularity she committed by pleading guilty instead of not guilty. This added detail was taken from elsewhere in the novel by Camus – no stranger to the games the law plays, as is shown by *L'Étranger* and *La Chute* – in order to heighten the suspense when the audience is waiting for Nancy's reaction to her sentence, and to start the play off with a punch in an atmosphere of outrage and disorder. To extract the maximum dramatic effect from an incident is much more important for a playwright than for a novelist. This is not to say that it does not matter at all for the latter; it is just that he has more time and more of the reader's imagination to play with than the dramatist. Camus demonstrates skill in reshaping other situations which, although quite adequately exploited in the novel, need to be more sharply focused on the stage. One incident is a complete interpolation on Camus's part. He has Temple's love letters passed on to her husband Gowan by Nancy (via the lawyer Gavin Stevens). Camus has thus made use of a material detail which Faulkner had allowed to fade out of the action altogether to create a climactic tension in the last act – will Gowan burn the letters without reading them? – which is dramatically powerful in its own right and at the same time serves the all-important function of placing greater emphasis on the character of Gowan.

Altogether the effect of Camus's streamlining of the plot and characterization is to turn *Requiem* much more into a well-contrived psychological drama, curiously, the sort of play which he normally abhorred. Inevitably the play has lost some of the spirit of the Faulkner novel. It was to be expected that in translation the play would fail to evoke the atmosphere of the American South, and Camus has in fact made no attempt to find French equivalents of Southern speech patterns. The problem of the dialogue was regarded by Camus as the most difficult aspect of the adaptation – but by no means because of this specific linguistic and cultural feature of the Mississippi background. His aim was the same as that announced in an earlier attempt to create modern tragedy, *Le Malentendu*, namely to contrive a style of dialogue which is 'natural enough to be spoken by our contemporaries and at the same time sufficiently different to be tragic'. Camus considered that Faulkner had solved the problem in English:

Or le style de Faulkner, avec son souffle saccadé, ses phrases interrompues, reprises et prolongées en répétitions, ses incidences, ses parenthèses et ses cascades de subordonnées, nous fournit un équivalent moderne, et nullement artificiel, de la tirade tragique. C'est un style qui halète, du halètement même de la souffrance. Une spirale, interminablement dévidée, de mots et de phrases conduit celui qui parle aux abîmes des souffrances ensevelies dans le passé . . . (*TRN*, p. 1859.)

At the same time he was of the opinion that an excessive use of this 'breathless' psychopathic naturalism could be both monotonous and melodramatic. Consequently he reserved it, or what he considered to be a French pastiche of it, for the emotional peaks of the play – 'tout ce qui concernait la souffrance nue, irrépressible, et particulièrement dans les aveux de Temple et les révoltes de son mari'. A comparison of the following passages demonstrates Camus's technique of breaking up an excessively long tirade in the crucial confession scene by means of remarks from the Governor or Gavin Stevens. At the same time it shows that, although Camus was principally obliged to cut speeches, he was nevertheless willing to expand a digression where he considered it appropriate. Above all Camus's text exemplifies his attempt to capture Faulkner's convoluted, paroxysmic style at moments of tension. The English passage is only the first half of one of Temple's tirades:

GOVERNOR. The young man died –
TEMPLE. Oh yes – Died, shot from a car while he was slipping up the alley behind the house, to climb up the same drainpipe I could have climbed down at any time and got away, to see me – the one time, the first time, the only time when we thought we had dodged, fooled him, could be alone together, just the two of us, after all the . . . other ones. – If love can be, mean anything, except the newness, the learning, the peace, the privacy: no shame: not even conscious that you are naked because you are just using the nakedness because that's a part of it; then he was dead, killed, shot down right in the middle of thinking about me, when in just one more minute maybe he would have been in the room with me, when all of him except just his body was already in the room

with me and the door locked at last just for the two of us alone; and then it was all over and as though it had never been, happened: it had to be as though it had never happened, except that that was even worse –

(*rapidly*)

Then the courtroom in Jefferson and I didn't care, not about anything any more, and my father and brothers waiting and then the year in Europe, Paris, and I still didn't care, and then after a while it really did get easier. You know. People are lucky. They are wonderful. At first you think that you can bear only so much and then you will be free. Then you find out that you can bear anything, you really can and then it won't even matter. Because suddenly it could be as if it had never been, never happened. You know: somebody – Hemingway, wasn't it? – wrote a book about how it had never actually happened to a gir– woman, if she just refused to accept it, no matter who remembered, bragged. And besides, the ones who could – remember – were both dead. Then Gowan came to Paris that winter and we were married – at the Embassy, with a reception afterwards at the Crillon.[5]

This becomes, in Camus's version:

LE GOUVERNEUR. Ce jeune homme, Red, de quoi est-il mort?
TEMPLE. De mort naturelle. Je veux dire conforme à sa nature. Il a été tué d'un coup de feu tiré d'une voiture pendant qu'il se faufilait dans une ruelle, derrière la maison, pour grimper dans ma chambre par le tuyau de descente. Oui, nous avions un rendez-vous clandestin, le premier que Popeye ne connût pas. Ce fut la première, la seule fois, où nous croyions avoir réussi à le tromper. Nous voulions être seuls, ensemble, rien que nous deux enfin, après toutes les fois, les autres fois, où nous ne l'étions pas. Nous avions enfin un rendez-vous d'amour. Car si l'amour peut exister, si ce mot peut avoir du sens, que signifie-t-il d'autre que la connaissance mutuelle

dans le silence, l'intimité, l'absence de honte? On ne s'aime pas quand on sait qu'on est nus. Et on sait qu'on est nus quand quelqu'un, au même moment, vous regarde. Alors nous voulions être seuls, au moins une fois, une seule fois, oublier tout ce qui n'était pas notre amour . . .

LE GOUVERNEUR. Votre amour? Red vous aimait-il?

TEMPLE. Il m'aimait. Peut-être parce que je l'aimais et qu'il ne s'y attendait pas, qu'il n'aurait jamais de lui-même pensé à une pareille histoire, imaginé ce qu'il appelait une chance, une telle chance, et il était là, devant moi, son maître derrière lui, et il me regardait, tremblant un peu, ne pouvant me parler des lettres que je lui envoyais en secret, silencieux d'ailleurs, parce qu'il savait qu'il ne pourrait maîtriser sa voix, mais son visage parlait et Popeye ne pouvait pas le voir. Oui, nous avons voulu vivre du moins une fois cet amour dont nous étions sûrs, et nous avons arrangé ce rendez-vous clandestin, notre lune de miel, si j'ose dire . . . Enfin, on l'a tué au moment où il venait seul vers moi seule! Il a été abattu à l'instant même où il pensait le plus à moi, et moi à lui, alors que peut-être, une minute plus tard, il eût été avec moi dans la même chambre, la porte fermée à clef, rien que nous deux enfin. Et ce fut fini. Ce fut comme si rien de tout cela, ni Red, ni la maison, ni les filles, ni Popeye n'avaient jamais existé. (*Elle parle plus vite.*) Ensuite, je suis revenue chez moi, quand Popeye a été arrêté pour ce meurtre, puis condamné à mort. Tout désormais m'était égal; et mon père et mes frères, là, à attendre. Et puis j'ai passé une année en Europe, à Paris. Là encore tout m'était égal.

STEVENS. Mais Gowan vint à Paris cet hiver-là et vous vous êtes mariés.

TEMPLE (*docilement*). Oui. A l'ambassade avec, ensuite, une réception au Crillon . . . (*TRN*, pp. 875-7.)

Both of Temple's speeches in Camus's version have a decided rhetorical effect in the theatre. However, a close comparison of, say, the first one with the corresponding passage in Faulkner reveals, as would many another in the play, that Camus's 'style haletant' has a very different character from the original. Falkner's asyntactic, semi-hermetic style with its non-sequiturs, its ellipses of auxiliary verbs, its repetition of 'then . . . then . . .' is translated into an articulate and coherent rhetoric, correct to the last parenthetic comma and even the imperfect subjunctive affected by Clamence in *La Chute*. When Temple says

> If love can be, mean anything, except the newness, the learning, the peace, the privacy: no shame: not even conscious that you are naked because you are just using the nakedness because that's a part of it . . .

Faulkner has no more need of correct syntax to convey Temple's meaning and the state of her mind than did Shakespeare when he portrayed Ophelia's madness. As Laertes put it: 'Hadst thou thy wits, and didst persuade revenge, It could not move thus.' Camus's Temple has her wits too much in evidence:

> Car si l'amour peut exister, si ce mot peut avoir du sens, que signifie-t-il d'autre que la connaissance mutuelle dans le silence, l'intimité, l'absence de honte?

Camus has eschewed the naturalistic rhythm and phrasing of Faulkner and substituted what one might term his own neo-classicism – stylized, harmonious, semi-poetic and basically unconversational dialogue which is almost Racinian in its lucidity and carefully controlled rhetoric. The impression is inescapable that Camus's characters, particularly Temple and Nancy, are more perceptive in their analysis of the situation which confronts them and more cogent in their utterance than Faulkner would ever wish them to be. 'Ce n'est pas une pièce, c'est un monde où j'ai introduit la logique. Pour le public français, le théâtre n'est pas concevable sans unité' (*TRN*, p. 1870) – such is Camus's view of *Requiem for a Nun* and of his part in adapting it. Can one cartesianize Faulkner? I think not. No more than one can cartesianize Dostoevsky, as we shall now see.

137

Camus claimed to owe more to Dostoevsky than to any other novelist. He played Ivan Karamazov in the Équipe production of *The Brothers Karamazov* ('il me semblait le comprendre parfaitement') and became increasingly haunted by the prophetic vision of this work and of *The Devils* throughout his career. It is difficult to imagine *L'Homme révolté* without the focus provided by the two Dostoevsky characters who, in Camus's view, dominate the nihilist evolution from Saint-Just to Stalin: Ivan Karamazov and Peter Verkhovensky. We have already seen in *Les Justes* what Camus, taking his cue from Dostoevsky, considered to be the political consequences of Ivan's anguishing hypothesis that if there is no divine sanction then anything is permissible. Stepan Fedorov was the prototype of the twentieth-century terrorist. Based on a historical event in 1905, *Les Justes* came exactly half-way between the formulation of the theory of Bakunin and Nechaev, and, as Camus saw it, the systematic application of it by the Communist autocrats of the USSR. Stalinism was constantly selected for attention by Camus at the time he was writing *L'Homme révolté*, but of course, as is shown by *L'État de siège*, all forms of modern tyranny and institutionalized terror and violence are included, on the right as well as on the left. Now with his adaptation of *The Devils* Camus moved back in time to the age of formulation and experiment. It is thus possible to speak of a historical trilogy, spanning the period 1860–1950: *Les Possédés, Les Justes, L'État de siège*, dealing with political nihilism and 'ses suites monstrueuses [et] les voies du salut'.

Like *Les Justes*, *The Devils* was based on a remarkable incident in Russian history. In 1869 and 1870 Dostoevsky was projecting a major novel condemning the whole corpus of progressive ideologies which had been imported into Russia since the time of the *Encyclopédie:* 'What I am writing now is a tendentious thing – I feel like saying everything as passionately as possible. (Let the nihilists and the Westerners scream that I am a *reactionary*!) To hell with them. I shall say everything to the last word.'[6] 'The last word' was that the various '-isms' of western Europe – atheism, agnosticism, deism, cosmopolitanism, socialism, liberalism, positivism, etc., were so many dangerous impurities inhabiting the body of Holy and mystic Russia like the devils in the sick man of St Luke's Gospel. The title of the work, 'The Devils', and the parabolic allusion to contemporary Russia are explained at the end of the novel when, in a moment of tragi-comic illumination, the elder Verkhovensky compares himself and others who have toyed with modern ideas to the Gadarene swine: 'They are we, we and them, and Peter – *et les autres avec lui*, and perhaps I at the head of them all, and we shall cast ourselves down, the raving and the possessed, from the cliff into the sea and shall all be drowned and serves us right, for that is all we are good for.' (*Devils*, p. 648.) Originally Dostoevsky toyed with the idea of calling the novel *The Atheist* since it had as its central figure a somewhat Byronic aristocrat who appears to have been the prototype of Stavrogin. On 21 November 1869, however, a student called Ivanov was murdered in Moscow by a small group of revolutionaries led by Nechaev. Although Nechaev was not brought to trial until 1873 all the facts were soon known. They were utilized immediately by Dostoevsky to form the basis of the murder of Shatov. He saw Nechaev, whose ruthlessness apparently proved too much even for Bakunin and Engels, as the sudden dramatic incarnation of the Western European Mephistopheles who had poisoned the soul of the Russian Faust. From this time onwards the bifurcation Verkhovensky-Stavrogin was clear in his mind.

Les Possédés, therefore, of the six translations or adaptations of the 1950s, is the one with the spirit of which Camus could most completely identify himself. One of the scenes which is most carefully transplanted from the novel into the play and which, together with the chapters entitled 'Trois Possédés' and 'Les Meurtriers Délicats', forms the basis of a whole section of *L'Homme révolté*, is that in which Shigalev, described as a 'fanatic lover of mankind', attempts to propound his system of world government: '. . . my conclusion is in direct contradiction to the original idea with which I start. Starting from unlimited freedom, I arrived at unlimited despotism, I will add, however, that there can be no other solution of the social formula than mine.' (*Devils*,

p. 404.) Shigalev's 'contradiction' lies in the fact that in order to put an end to injustice, principally the Tsarist oppression of the serfs, he can find no other solution than to create another order of injustice in which mankind would be divided into two groups: one-tenth would possess absolute power over the other nine-tenths. The latter will thus 'by their boundless obedience . . . and a series of regenerations attain a state of primeval innocence, something like the original paradise. They will have to work, however . . .' (Devils, p. 405.) Verkhovensky considers that Shigalev's discussion is in any case a waste of precious time:

> Disregarding all this talk – for we can't just go on talking for another thirty years as people have done for the last thirty – let me ask you which you prefer: the slow way consisting of the composition of social novels and the dry, unimaginative planning of the destinies of mankind a thousand years hence, while despotism swallows the morsels of roast meat which would fly into your mouths of themselves, but which you fail to catch; or are you in favour of a quick solution, whatever it may be, which will at last untie your hands and which will give humanity ample scope for ordering its own social affairs in a practical way and not on paper? They shout: a hundred million heads; well, that may be only a metaphor, but why be afraid of it if with the slow paper-dreams despotism will in a hundred or so years devour not a hundred but five hundred million heads? (Devils, p. 409.)

Verkhovensky represented the same evil for Dostoevsky and Camus: the fanaticism of the power-maniac. The basic premisses on which the two authors worked were slightly different, but not irreconcilable. They are explained by the two titles. In Dostoevsky's eyes Russia was the 'sick man' whose body was visited by the 'devils' of Western Enlightenment. These devils are the cause of this outbreak of anarchy and it is they which Dostoevsky wished to extirpate in his prophetic fashion by means of the parable of the Gadarene swine. For Camus, it was not the ideas which were anathema but the fanatics who claimed to serve them, while really gratifying their hatred, frustrated social ambition and lust for power. Camus's target is not the 'devils' but the more extreme of the 'possessed' themselves. The *limit* among the possessed falls between the older, bourgeois liberal humanist type, Stepan Verkhovensky, who is comically ineffectual but decent, and on the other hand his son: 'STEPAN: Ce ne sont pas mes idées. Tu [Pierre] veux tout détruire . . . Moi, je voulais que tout le monde s'aime.' (*TRN*, p. 993.)

It was the sheer technical difficulties which drew out the adaptation for such a long time after Camus made his first notes in the *Carnets* in 1953. In most editions *The Devils* is well over 600 pages long. It contains no fewer than fifty characters who participate in the action at some point or other, and the action furthermore is situated in a score of different places. There are many difficult 'ensemble' scenes, such as those in Barbara Stavrogin's salon, or at Virginsky's, in which characters of some significance to the novel as a whole (and therefore not dispensable) are left hanging with no dialogue or 'business' – a common problem for anyone who adapts a nineteenth-century novel for the stage. Other scenes of importance are of an epic nature, for example the Governor's Ball and the fire. Others, equally important, such as Barbara Stavrogin's encounter with Maria Lebyadkin outside the church, last only a minute or two and would not warrant a separate set in any type of conventional adaptation and style of production (such as Camus's) which depends on a certain degree of scenic realism. Finally, and supposing that the technical drawbacks to a production containing so many sets and characters can be surmounted, there is the whole question of tone. Dostoevsky's novels are characterized by great tension at times exploding in hysteria. This may be captured on film but with far less ease in the theatre unless frankly expressionistic techniques are used. The dramatist has at his disposal few of those means of arresting, focusing or titillating the imagination which are the camera's equivalent of the novelist's commentary or digression.

On the positive side there are certain inherent advantages in *The Devils* from an adaptor's point of view. Dostoevsky manifests a dramatist's instinct throughout. To begin with, the bulk of the novel consists of dialogue – Camus in fact had to interpolate very little. The movements of characters, their gestures and changes of tone are indicated briefly by Dostoevsky without extensive digression, as are the settings of all the scenes. The novel contains many incidents of an undoubted theatrical nature: Stavrogin's early outrages (inexplicably in the middle of company biting a man's ear and pulling another by the nose), Shatov's blow, his murder and the suicide of Kirilov, all these create considerable suspense of a legitimate kind – legitimate, that is, in a novel or play which is precisely about an epidemic of physical outrage in an otherwise sedate middle-class society.

When allowance is made for the advantages and disadvantages of the raw material the result is not altogether satisfactory. As in *Requiem*, Camus has generally been faithful to the letter, but has lost much of the spirit. In fairness to him, his technical ingenuity must be admired. Virtually the whole of the plot of *The Devils* is contained in twenty-two tableaux: only the Governor and his wife, and Karmazinov (a caricature of Turgenev) have been omitted of the principal characters, and the ballroom scene of the main set-pieces of action. Little of the basic plot of the novel is altered or omitted, and Dostoevsky's message is clearly presented. Perhaps this is the trouble. The issues are too clear. The main bearer of light is the omniscient and ironical narrator, Grigoreiev. Thus the 'mystery of Stavrogin' is no mystery at all: 'De qui cette malheureuse infirme était-elle la femme? Était-il vrai que Dacha avait été déshonorée et par qui? Qui encore avait séduit la femme de Chatov? Eh bien, nous allons recevoir une réponse!' (*TRN*, p. 969.) There is no need whatsoever for an answer because it has already been given. The first three tableaux have contained a large amount of discussion about Stavrogin's misconduct in St Petersburg and Switzerland and his relationship with Dacha,

Lisa and Mary Shatov: now, a few seconds before Grigoreiev's intervention, Captain Lebyadkin has been on the point of revealing the identity of his sister's 'Prince', her lawful husband in fact. Nowhere in the novel did Dostoevsky link the names of the three women in such a pointed manner as Camus above: this would have been quite destructive to the atmosphere of perplexity he wished to create. Camus might have made exactly the same statement about *Les Possédés* that he made about his part in *Requiem* – a world where he had introduced logic to satisfy the classical French demand for unity in the theatre.

Inevitably, much of the epic presentation of Tsarist society on the brink of chaos has disappeared. The atmosphere of imminent social and individual paroxysm, which is a vital element in the novel, has subsided. Part of the responsibility for this must lie with the stiff, orthodox structure of Camus's play, respecting logical time-sequences, making no allowance for a more subjective use of lighting, décor, sound, or crowd scenes to capture the true atmosphere of the novel. If Camus's use of the stage fails to do justice to the feverishness and spontaneous violence of *The Devils*, his dialogue fails even more. The difference between the original dialogue and Camus's version is as great as it was in *Requiem for a Nun* but is perhaps more detrimental now, since Dostoevsky relies on dialogue to satirize many of his characters, particularly the nihilists. In *The Devils* they express themselves with a quirky Dickensian garrulousness mixed with a rather humourless Slav intensity, an idiom which Dostoevsky handles brilliantly to show up the gulf between their breathtaking pretensions and their ability. This disparity is all too easily exploited by a cynic like Verkhovensky: 'All right, here we are. [to Stavrogin, as they approach Virginsky's house for the meeting] Assume the right expression, Stavrogin. I always do when I go in. Try to look as grim as possible. That's all you need. It's very simple really.' (*Devils*, p. 389.)

This is how the men and women who propose to reorganize the whole world begin their business, in the French translation used by Camus:[7]

– Soit! grogna Liamchine. Il se mit au piano et commença à jouer une valse en tapant sur les touches comme un sourd, presque au petit bonheur.

– 'Je propose que ceux qui sont pour les séances lèvent la main,' dit Mme Virguinsky.

Les uns levèrent la main, les autres ne bougèrent pas. Il y en eut aussi qui levèrent la main puis la baissèrent pour la relever de nouveau.

'Au diable! je n'ai rien compris! s'écria l'un des officiers.

– Moi non plus, fit un autre.

– Mais si, je comprends, cria un troisième, si c'est *oui* on lève la main.

– Mais que signifie *oui*?

– Que vous êtes pour la séance.

– Pas du tout, au contraire.

– J'ai voté la séance, cria le collégien à Mme Virguinsky.

– Pourquoi alors n'avez-vous pas levé la main?

– Je vous ai regardé: vous ne l'avez pas levée, alors je ne l'ai pas levée non plus.

– C'est stupide! Je n'ai pas levé la main parce que je faisais voter. Messieurs, je propose une contre-épreuve: que celui qui est pour la séance reste immobile et ne lève pas la main; que celui qui est contre, lève la main droite.

Celui qui est contre? redemanda le collégien.

– Est-ce que vous le faites exprès? s'écria, furieuse, Mme Virguinsky.

– Non, permettez! qui doit lever la main? est-ce celui qui est pour ou contre? Il faut le dire clairement, firent quelques voix.

– Celui qui est contre, *contre.*

– Oui, mais que doit-il faire, lever la main ou ne pas la lever? cria un officier.

– Hé, hé! nous n'avons pas encore l'habitude du parlement, observa le major.

– Monsieur Liamchine, excusez-moi, mais vous faites un tel tapage que l'on ne s'entend plus, dit le professeur boiteux.'

In Camus the tone of the opening section of this key scene is quite different. Not only does he omit this masterful parody of the democratic process but he substitutes urbane exchanges in the crisp and articulate language which is used throughout the play and which is nowhere more inappropriate than here:

LE SÉMINARISTE. Messieurs, je n'ai pas l'habitude de perdre mon temps. Puisque vous avez eu la bonté de m'inviter à cette réunion, oserais-je poser une question?

LIPOUTINE. Osez, mon cher, osez. Vous jouissez ici de la sympathie générale depuis cette bonne farce que vous avez faite à la colporteuse en mélangeant des photographies obscènes à ses évangiles.

LE SÉMINARISTE. Ce n'est pas une farce. Je l'ai fait par conviction, étant d'avis qu'il faut fusiller Dieu.

LIPOUTINE. Est-ce là ce qu'on apprend au séminaire?

LE SÉMINARISTE. Non. Au séminaire, on souffre à cause de Dieu. Donc, on le hait. En tout cas voici ma question: sommes-nous, oui ou non, en séance?

CHIGALEV. Je constate que nous continuons à parler pour ne rien dire. Les responsables peuvent-ils nous dire pourquoi nous sommes là? (*TRN*, p. 1045.)

In view of Camus's faithfulness to the plot and characterization of *The Devils*, and his admiration for the Spanish and Elizabethan theatre, in which (as indeed in the 'Russian temperament' according to cliché) tears and laughter are constantly intermingled, it is curious that he should have been so insensitive to Dostoevsky's tragi-comic vision in so far as it is inherent in his dialogue. It is curious too that he should not have attempted to find French equivalents for the highly individualized styles of expression which Dostoevsky creates for all his characters. When, in Dostoevsky, the passionately incoherent and lugubrious Shigalev expounds his doctrine he meets with laughter and incomprehension. In Camus he is eloquent, poised and ironic:

> Oui. C'est ainsi que j'obtiens l'égalité. Tous les hommes sont esclaves et égaux dans l'esclavage. Autrement, ils ne peuvent être égaux. Donc, il faut niveler. On abaissera par exemple le niveau de l'instruction et des talents. Comme les hommes de talent veulent toujours s'élever, il faudra malheureusement arracher la langue de Cicéron, crever les yeux de Copernic et lapider Shakespeare. Voilà mon système. (*TRN*, p. 1049.)

What was comic naïvety in Dostoevsky is cynicism in Camus. The speech is worthy of Skouratov, Clamence or Hélicon, and indeed, in its perverse logic, it is reminiscent of the latter's 'petit traité de l'exécution'. Similarly with other characters the speech mannerisms, quirks and subtle tones which account for so much of the rich texture of this novel are ironed out into a polished, neo-classical discourse which does little justice to the genius of Dostoevsky.

Of the six translations and adaptations of this period, *Les Possédés* is clearly the most important for two reasons. It is after all the only one of the six which Camus had to create *as a play*, since *Requiem for a Nun* already existed in a reasonably acceptable dramatic form, and the other four plays required only varying degrees of modification. As such, therefore, *Les Possédés* tells us just as much as *Les Justes* and *Caligula* from the formal point of view about Camus's ability to fashion a viable dramatic text out of historical or semi-historical accounts of terrorism and murder, as presented by three very partial writers. In *Les Possédés* he demonstrates the same skill as he did in his two best original plays in building up tension by means of a series of climaxes, but at the same time reveals a preference for a rather conservative form, and above all for a highly stylized dialogue. Secondly, by virtue of implicitly endorsing Dostoevsky's prophetic vision of the Stalinist mentality, the play acts, as it were, as Camus's last will and testament. *Les Possédés* is his final denunciation of revolutionary nihilism, and the work to which he attached the most importance during the decade after *L'Homme révolté*. It is thus fitting that Camus's lifelong struggle against fanaticism should end, as it began, in the theatre.

8 Conclusion and Synthesis

Pour le drame, je ne lui vois d'autre maître que lui-même.

Rachel Bespaloff

It was shortly after seeing a performance of *Les Possédés* during its provincial tour that Camus was killed. Those close to him believe that at this time he was just emerging from his long and difficult period of sterility and reappraisal – he is known to have been working hard on a novel, *Le Premier Homme*, for example. As far as the theatre is concerned, he confided to Germaine Brée in 1959 that he was toying with the idea of a play linking Don Juan-Sganarelle and Faust-Mephistopheles which he regarded as 'two aspects of the same dichotomy'. But it seems certain that no fragment of this or any other late work for the theatre by Camus exists. All that is certain is that at the time of his death Camus was being lined up by André Malraux to take over a state-owned Parisian theatre to do experimental work within the national cultural scheme. Camus was only forty-six at the time of his death – an age at which Giraudoux, for example, had only just started to write for the theatre. Whether, once the Algerian War was over, and with his own theatre to work in amid the very different theatrical atmosphere of the 1960s, Camus would have gone on to produce a quantity of work of any significance makes interesting speculation, but is in the last resort doubtful. And so what finally is to be our assessment of the Camus whose last completely original work for the theatre was performed in 1949? Few critics, and even fewer theatre people, now believe that Camus's plays will enjoy the viability which seems assured for the work of dramatists such as Shaw, O'Casey, Pirandello, Brecht and Anouilh, although this stature appeared within Camus's

148

grasp after the success of *Les Justes*. Two questions must be asked: to what extent has Camus succeeded in creating the modern tragedy with which he was obsessed throughout his career, and how successful is his work *as theatre*, independently of whether it constitutes a convincing form of modern tragedy?

In answer to the first question, it seems to me that Camus does not make a really effective dramatic exploitation of the advantages which his political and philosophical theories would appear to give him. These, as expounded in 'L'Avenir de la tragédie', we examined in detail when discussing *Les Justes*. A predilection for the tragic theme of a conflict between a powerful individual (e.g. Antigone) and an invincible order, or representative of order (e.g. Creon), and a passionate concern for the importance of not transcending limits, more or less equating to the classical horror of *hubris* – overweening pride or *démesure* – these would appear to leave Camus just as richly endowed in dramatic theory as Corneille and Racine. And so they do. But Camus's practice is not really a logical extension in dramatic terms of his theory. His theatre has the absurd as its premiss, and this fact has far greater dramatic significance than the actions which result from it on the stage. Even if one agrees with Guicharnaud that Camus's plays, like those of Sartre, are 'crammed with action or the expectation of action',[1] the fact remains that his tragedy is one of situation. It is metaphysical not psychological, and as John Cruickshank has observed, does not present 'flawed' heroes in the Elizabethan sense. Camus was convinced – strangely so in an experienced man of the theatre who revered Sophocles and Shakespeare – that metaphysics and psychology were incompatible in tragedy; and for him psychology in fact was anathema in any guise in any sort of play.

Unfortunately this conception of metaphysical tragedy has resulted in an excessively abstract form of expression. One of the best examples of this is Camus's handling of the mask, a favourite theatrical device of French dramatists since the Renaissance. The physical object, originally inherited from the *commedia dell'arte* with its literal and concrete functions still intact (as an easily exploitable aid to intrigue), was soon conceptualized and used in a symbolic manner in the seventeenth and eighteenth centuries by Molière and Marivaux. *Préciosité, marivaudage,* fashion, and social and philosophical systems served as masks behind which vulnerable human beings took shelter. In this century Giraudoux and Anouilh in particular have been inspired by a new Italian stimulus, that of Pirandello, to make a consistent and dramatically compelling use of this technique. Discussing Camus's work in this respect, Thomas Bishop draws attention to *Caligula*. I have already stressed the importance of Cherea's remark 'on ne peut pas aimer celui de ses visages qu'on essaie de masquer en soi' and suggested why Camus has him stab Caligula specifically in the face. Bishop considers the crucial confrontation between the two men to be notable for its Pirandellian character:

> The references to masks concealing the reality of a person, to Cherea's several faces, to the pretence in the relations between people, are very reminiscent of the Italian dramatist. Whether they stem from Camus' knowledge of Pirandello cannot be determined, but they are certainly attributable to him indirectly, for these had, by 1945, become thoroughly naturalized in the French theater.[2]

This example, in *Caligula*, is the only one in Camus's theatre discussed by Bishop. In fact a thorough study reveals scores of allusions to the mask in its various forms. The mask, the instrument of inscrutability, the totally impenetrable screen around the personality, and cause of doubt, misunderstanding and murder, is the perfect metaphor of the absurd. In *Le Malentendu*, the blackest of his plays, Camus implies that this is the natural order of the world:

MARTHA. . . . car c'est maintenant que nous sommes dans l'ordre. Il faut vous en persuader.

MARIA. Quel ordre?

MARTHA. Celui où personne n'est jamais reconnu. (*TRN,* p. 178.)

This vision of a world in which 'no one is ever recognized' dominates all four plays. It should be noted that in each one Camus makes a very sparing literal use of the mask – some form of disguise or game of pretence. Caligula disguises himself as Venus; Kaliayev (off stage) as a street-hawker; Jan assumes the name of Karl Hasek; and Diego wears 'le masque des médecins de la peste'. There is, however, a considerable disparity between the brief and functional uses of the mask at a literal level and its application at the metaphorical level to stress the impossibility of communication, understanding and love between human beings. It is not just in *Le Malentendu* that Camus presents a despairing picture of a world in which the normal persona of human beings is the mask of tragedy. Once the mask is in place, it stays on. Only once does Camus manage effectively to exteriorize the transformation which has befallen the wearer, and that is in the powerful Act I curtain to *Caligula*. Before his assembled patricians and Caesonia, Caligula frantically 'rubs out' his old image in his mirror; thereafter he has 'le regard fixe':

> Plus rien, tu vois. Plus de souvenirs, tous les visages enfuis! Rien, plus rien. Et sais-tu ce qui reste? Approche encore. Regarde. Approchez. Regardez.
>
> (*Il se campe devant la glace dans une attitude démente.*)
>
> CAESONIA (*regardant le miroir, avec effroi*). Caligula!
>
> (*Caligula change de ton, pose son doigt sur la glace et, le regard soudain fixe, dit d'une voix triomphante*):
>
> CALIGULA. Caligula.   (*TRN*, pp. 24–30.)

In all four original plays once the mask has been put on human relations with even the closest associates are severed. And in *Les Possédés*, too, Stavroguine wears a mask (*le regard impassible, l'air rêveur et maussade, son visage pâle et sévère, comme pétrifié* – stressed on numerous occasions by Camus) and has done so ever since the day when the fact of the absurdity of the world penetrated his consciousness – when he was responsible for the death of the child Matriocha. The heroines object bitterly to the disguise their menfolk have assumed:

> (i) VICTORIA. . . . Je déteste ce visage de peur et de haine qui t'est venu!
> (ii) CAESONIA. . . . Je te reconnais mal.
> (iii) DORA. Je n'aime pas les déguisements.
> (iv) MARIA. . . . il suffirait de parler. Dans ces cas-là, on dit: 'C'est moi', et tout rentre dans l'ordre . . . il aurait suffi d'un mot.

But they cannot tear off the mask. In each play it either slips or is taken off temporarily (Caligula and Stavroguine both play what Caligula calls 'le jeu de la sincérité'), but is soon clamped back on after it has become apparent that alienation is irrevocable. The best example of this is Kaliayev's parting line to Dora: 'Au revoir. Je . . . La Russie sera belle.' Thus Dora's plea, 'Non, il faut bien une fois au moins laisser parler son cœur', which has an almost identical echo in each play, has a short-lived response. Dora, herself masked from this moment onwards, can only echo Kaliayev's robot-like 'La Russie sera belle.' The normal state of impenetrability returns in each play: 'JAN: . . . nous voilà revenus à nos conventions. MARTHA: Oui, et nous avons eu tort de nous en écarter.' This has been a desperate but futile attempt to re-establish human contact between those in whom it ought to be most natural: lovers (Kaliayev and Dora, Diego and Victoria), brother and sister (Jan and Martha) and 'deux hommes dont l'âme et la fierté sont égales' (Caligula and Cherea). This temporary slipping of the mask is the climax of each play. After this the way is clear for the dénouement in which the face behind the mask will in turn assume the rigour of death:

> DORA. Orlov a-t-il rencontré son regard?
> STEPAN. Non.
> DORA. Que regardait-il?

STEPAN. Tout le monde, dit Orlov, sans rien voir. (*TRN*, p. 389.)

In *Le Malentendu* it is Martha who plays the dominant role in this respect, but at the end of *Les Justes* Dora is similarly defeminized and transformed (*d'une voix changée*) when she justifies her demand to play the role of killer vacated by Kaliayev: 'Suis-je une femme maintenant?'

An awareness of Camus's idea of how the fact of the absurd can affect the human personality is thus essential for an understanding of the structure of his plays. Every main character from the first, Pèpe, to the last, Stavroguine, has become literally and metaphorically *figé*, fixed, blocked in time. In this respect – and coincidentally and not at all as a result of any 'influence' – Camus is perhaps more fundamentally Pirandellian than the scores of French dramatists who have made such ostentatious use of the Italian's more superficial plotting and characterization techniques since 1923. The trouble is that he hardly ever succeeds in rendering the mask/absurd metaphor concrete on the stage. The skill with which Anouilh, Giraudoux and Sartre manipulate *personae* is lacking in Camus, if not actually repugnant to him. One feels that Camus's commitment to his thesis – that alienation imposes masks of deception and insensitivity upon the real self – was too sincere. He was not dispassionate enough to use this classic device in a way which might legitimately please and intrigue in the theatre. Criticism after criticism of Camus's theatre offers the opinion that it is 'too intellectual', too obviously the work of a desiccated manipulator of ideas. On the contrary, the converse might just as easily be argued. Camus is indeed an intellectual dramatist in the sense that he believed the theatre ought to be a serious and non-commercial affair, a medium for important statements about the human condition, but hardly an intellectual in the matter of form. He does not possess the ability to stand back from his theme and present it objectively by means of illusion, perspective, juxtaposition of details in the classic manner of French dramatists since the seventeenth century. It is significant that two of Camus's

F

plays which are considered to be among the most successful, *Requiem pour une nonne* and *Les Possédés*, are adaptations which retain most of the 'popular' elements of the original novels: physical violence, mystery, dramatic irony, flashbacks. Camus could not avoid the action which is a key feature of the scenarios provided by Faulkner and Dostoevsky, although he did, as we have seen, create a very different atmosphere in each case. I doubt whether, if he had lived to begin a new cycle of plays in the 1960s, Camus would have learned the lesson of these successes, namely that his ideal modern tragedy need not be static, totally verbal and interior. For Camus's abhorrence of technical virtuosity, psychological theatre and the well-made play stem from an intellectual disdain on his part which made him equate popular and 'theatrical' elements with inferior theatre. Camus was handicapped by a certain puritanism which reminds one of Copeau. He did in fact refer to 'ces moines', je veux dire [les] gens de théâtre' (*TRN*, p. 1720) and Blanche Balain has described the moral earnestness of the Équipe during Camus's formative years: 'Je fus frappée certains soirs par une pureté de l'atmosphère intellectuelle et morale qui venait elle-même d'une certaine vigueur et d'une certaine passion habitant les meilleurs d'entre nous.' (*TRN*, p. 1691.)

The best-known of the pronouncements Camus made criticizing all departures from his own idea of a stringent, sombre, tragic theatre is his early article on Giraudoux, whom he regarded as 'l'un des écrivains les moins faits pour le théâtre'. What Camus objected to was a self-conscious dramatic form where the intellect, as opposed to the emotion, of the dramatist was to the fore:

> L'afféterie a fait son œuvre. Si la grâce, l'esprit, le conventionnel et le charmant peuvent convenir à la rigueur au roman, ils sont la négation même du théâtre . . . L'intelligence ici ne sert qu'elle-même et c'est en vain qu'on attend, qu'on espère et qu'on poursuit un peu de cette chaleur humaine et de cette divine passion qui nous faisait aimer également Hamlet et Iago. (*TRN*, p. 1408.)

At the same stage of his career Camus expressed similar misgivings about Gide's *Le Roi Candaule:* 'L'art dramatique est fatal aux subtilités de l'intelligence.' In view of his strictures about stressing *forme* at the expense of *fond*, and particularly the intellect at the expense of the emotions, it is paradoxical that one of the earliest critics of *Caligula* regrets the same disequilibrium, but this time at Camus's expense:

> On peut faire à cette pièce le reproche souvent fait aux pièces de Giraudoux: l'émotion ressentie est une émotion de l'intelligence, ce n'est pas une émotion de la sensibilité. *Sodome et Gomorrhe* bouleversait notre intelligence et laissait notre cœur intact, alors que l'*Antigone* d'Anouilh s'adressait à notre cœur. Caligula n'est pas un homme, c'est un système philosophique.[3]

Camus in fact defined the play as a 'tragedy of the intelligence' but made repeated attempts in the successive versions to make the play more human by modifying and developing the characters of Hélicon and Scipion for example, and making the character of Caligula more sympathetic. And yet, as Albert Sonnenfeld has argued in a detailed discussion of Camus's 'failure' as a dramatist, it is very difficult for the audience to establish contact on any sort of human level with the hero. The problem is the one we examined in connection with *Le Malentendu*, that of communicating to an audience the real experience of the absurd, one of the effects of which is the impossibility of communicating anything to anyone. The task is feasible *à la rigueur* in the novel or cinema, but not in the theatre, as Martin Esslin has argued, unless the dramatist adopts a radically 'anti-cartesian' approach to dialogue, characterization and dramatic structure.[4] Although I have tried to show how, just for one moment, Camus appeared to be on the verge of a breakthrough with the character of 'le Vieux', the problem is one which he did not make any consistent attempt to solve. The highly experimental (and brilliantly successful) prose style of *L'Étranger* has no counterpart in the plays. Split asunder by this gulf between form and theme, Camus's theatre constitutes one of the greatest paradoxes of the transitional decade 1940–50.

The emphasis so far in this Conclusion has been on some of the characteristics of Camus's theatre which are more conveniently discussed in a general survey than in the chapters devoted to the individual plays. The time has now come to make a résumé of the main aspects of Camus's dramatic style, making allowance for the difficulty of synthesizing the work of such a highly personal artist who never repeated the exact theme and form of any work, either in the theatre or in any other medium.

Taking theme first, all of Camus's original plays and most of those he adapted or translated are based in some measure on the premiss that our human condition is absurd. Violence and repression are common features. The inevitability of death is a source of unparalleled anguish (*Caligula*), as is the arrogation of the power of life and death over other people (*Les Justes*, *Requiem pour une nonne*). Even when enjoying social and material success, man is haunted by an eternal quest for some physical or metaphysical goal, the exact nature of which is not always clear to him (*Le Malentendu*). Chance frequently takes what seems to be almost a malevolent course, thwarting all attempts to achieve happiness (*Le Malentendu*) or arbitrarily destroying that which already exists (*Caligula*). The protagonists are generally alienated from their physical background and from those human beings one would expect to be closest to them (*Le Malentendu*, *Un Cas intéressant*). The fact of the absurd can strike not merely individuals but whole sections of society. Civilized society is then split asunder in a conflict characterized by cowardice and treachery, and nihilistic collaboration with the absurd (*L'État de siège*, *Révolte dans les Asturies*, *Les Possédés*).

All of Camus's plays are based on conflict. The manifestations of the absurd constitute one of the terms – the general condition or existing order, against which the heroes of Camus's plays react, or rebel. The heroes, the antithetical term, are animated by a sense of 'revolt'. In *Le Mythe de Sisyphe* revolt designated a state of spiritual tension based on a lucid scrutiny of the absurd, and culminated in a curious form of stoic happiness. But in the theatre Camus handles revolt in a much more moralistic manner. Revolt must be creative and relative, not destructive and absolute (revolution). It must be based on a recognition of values, a 'qualitative' ethic, that is to say a scale of ethical priorities involving the totality of mankind. The rebel may not therefore combat the absurd with all the means at his disposal, and must be prepared for the anguish of making value-judgements about other people, whose claims to life are no less great than his own. At all times the rebel must be aware of a *limit*, beyond which he must not pass, on pain of redeeming transgression with his own life. And yet the absurd presents a terrifying paradox. It is in itself a total experience: life is never the same again. People of intelligence and sensitivity are tempted to make a total reaction, since the 'logic' of the absurd in the mind of whoever fully experiences it requires that the whole basis of society be transformed and an awareness of the absurd be universalized. This is the temptation of the 'tout ou rien'; the absurd is difficult to live with. The tension it creates is the centre of the tragic dilemma of each play.

The form that Camus's plays take is conditioned by these linked themes of the absurd and revolt. At its most profound level of interpretation Camus's theatre is metaphysical tragedy in which a basically noble and sensitive individual is pitted against an invincible and inscrutable order. It is characterized by a state of tension which is frequently independent of what happens during the course of the play. As a representation of human action on the other hand, Camus's theatre is strictly speaking not tragedy in any recognized formal sense so much as melodrama according to his own definition: a simplistic presentation of right and wrong. This explains the heroic and Romantic aura of much of his characterization. Theme dominates form: what the play is saying is more important than the way in which it says it. Camus has no time for theatrical games. He has something to say and he gets on with it. His characteristic plot is therefore linear, situated on the brink of a crisis, and is developed in a straightforward and chronological manner.

Settings are likewise simple and economical, and are not intended to evoke the physical and historical atmosphere of Imperial Rome, Tsarist Moscow, mid-twentieth-century Czechoslovakia or Spain with any precision. Thus *Le Malentendu* might just as easily be set in a landlocked province of Canada or Russia, and *L'État de siège* in Lisbon or Naples. The essential details are the north/south and land/sea dichotomies which have so much importance everywhere in Camus's work and also in his own life. As a general rule in the successive drafts of his plays Camus attempted to de-particularize the setting and/or historical circumstances of the plot, manifesting an almost classical French concern for stylization in this respect.

In characterization, too, Camus shows the same tendency to stress general rather than particular features. This explains the inescapable impression of rigidity that many of Camus's characters make. Rather than individuals they represent types of social and philosophical positions: revolt (Diego, Pèpe, Kaliayev), 'revolution' (Stepan, Caligula, Martha), cynical nihilism (Nada, Skouratov, Hélicon), proletarian indifference (Foka), vile bourgeoisie (the judge, the grocer, the chemist), the eternal feminine (Dora, Maria, Caesonia, Victoria, Pilar), the young idealist making his first contact with reality (Scipion, Voinov), the mature relativist (Cherea, Annenkov) . . . the list could continue until every character in Camus's theatre is categorized.

Camus's dialogue is consistent with this philosophical conception of character and setting. He regarded language as the main problem in modern tragedy, and sought to create a stylized, neutral idiom which would nevertheless be recognizable as the language of the twentieth century and yet at the same time sufficiently 'distanced' and elevated to create what he considered to be the proper aura of tragedy. With the exception of his immature apprentice-piece, *Révolte dans les Asturies*, his dialogue is polished, correct, even literary. In his search for modern tragedy Camus had no time for naturalism, and, much though he was affected by Hemingway and Faulkner in the novel, one feels he would have wished to derive nothing at all from their fellow

American Arthur Miller in the theatre. Pèpe, calling his grocer 'con', 'fumier', 'ordure', finds no echo in Camus's mature theatre. Camus is 'correct' to the extent of using totally unnaturalistic structures such as the past historic, imperfect subjunctive and the inverted form of the interrogative. Thus at the height of her extremely emotional confession Temple Drake can say 'Mais Gowan *vint* à Paris' and 'il *eût* été avec moi'. Annenkov is just as formal: '. . . il fallait que tout *fût* prévu et que personne ne *pût* hésiter sur ce qu'il y avait à faire.' In fact *Les Justes* provides some good examples of Camus's style of dialogue. An important index of popular speech is the syntax of the interrogative. The characters are almost completely consistent in their use of inversion of the subject and verb (e.g. *est-il prêt?*) where naturalism would have demanded one of the far more common structures without inversion: *il est prêt?*, *est-ce qu'il est prêt?* Unlike Sartre or Anouilh, Camus makes little or no concession to popular usage. Thus the Guard in *Antigone*, with his 'Et à qui qu'elle est adressée?' contrasts with Camus's Foka: 'Combien en as-tu tué?' and 'Que fait-on à ceux qui tuent les grands-ducs?' The use of inversion is even more striking in Stepan. He is aggressively anti-bourgeois, functional and uncultured – the sort of person who loathes eloquence. But we know this from *what* he says, not from *how* he says it. For in the opening scene of the play he strikes a formal note from the very beginning with three successive questions: 'Tout est-il prêt, Boria?', 'La proclamation est-elle rédigée?' and 'Que dois-je faire?', which all indicate Camus's avoidance of truly popular idiom. It is not strictly true that Camus makes no concessions at all in Foka's dialogue. He makes some: 'Le grand-duc? Eh, comme tu y vas. Voyez-vous ces barines! C'est grave, dis-moi?' But he still holds back from a full use of the popular phrasing, slang, interjections, elisions, epentheses, etc., which a dramatist like Sartre gives to most comparable characters in his plays. Once again Stepan is a good illustration of Camus's stylization in this respect. He makes only the slightest possible recognition of the difference of character and background. He gives Stepan dialogue which shows a certain vigour and lack of circumlocution:

Est-ce que vous vous rendez compte de ce que signifie cette décision? Deux mois de filatures, de terribles dangers courrus et évités, deux mois perdus à jamais. Egor arrêté pour rien. Rikov perdu pour rien. Et il faudrait recommencer? Encore de longues semaines de veilles et de ruses, de tension incessante, avant de retrouver l'occasion propice? Êtes-vous fous? (*TRN*, pp. 334–5.)

However, it contains no coarseness or popular features, and displays a vocabulary and articulateness ('tension incessante', 'l'occasion propice') which lift the character off the plane of the *real* pre-revolutionary Moscow of 1905. There are no particularizing features in the dialogue of the other characters either. Kaliayev, Dora, Boris and Voinov speak to each other as they would to Foka or the Grand Duchess, showing none of the familiarity, jargon or slang which might evoke an intimate milieu of middle- and lower-middle-class students and intellectuals of around 1900, either in Russia or anywhere else. And in fact throughout his mature theatre, with the slight exception of Foka, Camus makes no recognition of class or regional usage, even where it would be in order or is to be found in the source material (Nancy Mannigoe, Stepan Fedorov, Fedka) or where a flow of polished, neo-classical discourse would appear to be inappropriate – in Martha and her mother, who are meant to be 'une jeune fille au langage net' and a semi-literate old peasant woman. He eschewed individualization of dialogue and naturalistic speech patterns as much as he did 'psychological' characterization and specific physical and geographical settings.

Camus thus tried to harmonize all the elements of form to accord with his metaphysical and somewhat abstract themes. The universal and symbolic implications of his plays are stressed at the expense of the historical and concrete. With their elevated and unified tone, purity of language, minimization of physical detail, and concentration upon theme to the exclusion of superfluous humour, anecdote and scenic ingenuity, Camus's plays are thus much more authentically classical in form than those of his contemporaries. And yet there is always something lacking too. That vital spark of human warmth, of truly theatrical tension when a dramatist who is the complete master of his effects grips his audience exactly as he wishes through his characters, glows sporadically in *Le Malentendu* and *Les Justes* and perhaps comes near to being sustained only in *Caligula*. Despite the fact that, given the right production in the right place, these three plays can and occasionally do work well (and even *L'État de siège* appears to have had its moments in German translation), it remains true that in the last resort Camus's theatre reads far better than it acts. Thus by the standards the author set himself it is unsatisfactory, not to say a failure. I think it is possible to account for this, in summary, by pointing to half a dozen factors:

(1) Camus never really solved the problem of communicating the feeling of the absurd in the theatre. In search of this, his experiments in stylization of form led him totally in the wrong direction – into an impasse from which he could have broken out only by abandoning his cartesian approach to language and structure.

(2) In his three conscious attempts at creating modern tragedy, *Le Malentendu*, *Les Justes* and *L'État de siège*, Camus failed to harmonize form and theme. The important elements of *hamartia*, peripeteia and anagnorisis (particularly the latter pair) are lacking in *Les Justes* and *L'État de siège*: Diego and Kaliayev die too well and too willingly. *Le Malentendu* on the other hand, as the title of the play suggests, is shot through with peripeteia, the tragic irony of recoil, but Jan dies unconscious, and the anagnorisis is reserved for two characters who were not originally conceived by Camus as the central tragic figures, Jan's mother and sister. Camus's plays are frequently considered to be 'well-constructed and polished' (Esslin), but in so far as they are attempts to recapture the spirit of tragedy this appearance is deceptive, for they lack its essential structural consistency or unity of action. Where they are 'tragic' – as metaphysical situation – they are not dramatic; and where they are dramatic – as representation of human action – they are not tragic. The play in which Camus comes closest to capturing the

real feel of classical tragedy is the one in which he is least consciously trying to concoct it, the one in which he creates not a twentieth-century everyman but a Nietzschean superhuman, Caligula.

(3) Although he was the most theatre-conscious and experienced of the French novelist-playwrights, Camus was surprisingly loath to employ the full resources of the modern theatre, and had an uncertain command of dramatic effects. Three pieces of crucial action are *narrated* in *Les Justes*; a borrowing from melodrama in *Le Malentendu* ('Will he or won't he drink the fatal potion?', etc.) is dramatically embarrassing in its context. The one consistent concession to theatricality, *L'État de siège*, is a badly organized series of sketches with no interior dramatic movement of its own.

(4) The philosophical and metaphysical implications of the plays are not fully clear to the average spectator without some foreknowledge of Camus's essays, his theory of tragedy and attitude to nihilism and dialectical materialism.

(5) During the immediate post-war years Camus's political commitment, particularly his increasingly passionate anti-Stalinism, got the better of his artistic judgement. Thus *L'État de siège* and *Les Justes* are marred by didacticism in almost every scene. As plays about twentieth-century political dilemmas – notwithstanding, paradoxically, the historical authenticity of *Les Justes* and the topicality of *L'État de siège* – they convince us far less than a play like *Les Mains sales*. Sartre paints politics as it is; Camus paints politics as it ought to be.

(6) Camus's concept of theatre is excessively verbal, yet fails to achieve a distinctive style of its own in any of the principal functions of language. Camus placed as great a reliance on the power of the spoken word as some of the great stylists of the French theatre: Corneille, Racine, Marivaux, Giraudoux and Beckett, and at times he reveals adroitness in his handling of rhetoric, lyricism (the choruses of *L'État de siège*), irony, wit and ambiguity. Yet he does not excel consistently in any of these forms of language in the theatre. He has nothing to offer of his

own beyond an impeccably well-phrased and stylized discourse which is surprisingly unoriginal in the author of *Noces* and *L'Étranger*. It is the ideal language of the moralist, of the man who is convinced that Kaliayev is right and Stepan is wrong, and wishes us to share his conviction. It is in fact the language of the novelist, but of the novelist who wrote *La Peste* and *La Chute* rather than *L'Étranger*.

Incommunicable metaphysics, disparity of form and theme, faulty theatrical judgement, philosophical complexity and abstraction, cloying didacticism and failure to develop a sufficiently personal and artistically appropriate language to bear the weight of the play: these are the principal criticisms of Camus's theatre. Yet it would be quite wrong to regard it as a total failure. Like other 'difficult' theatre – that of Claudel, for example – Camus's theatre possesses an undoubted resilience and a tendency, *given the right production*, to succeed at moments which seem frankly unstageworthy on the printed page. *Les Justes, Le Malentendu* and *Caligula* all have their champions, but the crucial reservation must always be 'given the right production'. This requires carefully stylized movement, lighting, grouping, gesture and delivery to establish a total *rapport* between actor and audience. The surest way to make plays like *Le Malentendu* and *Les Justes* fail is to play them apologetically like naturalism that has gone wrong. This is not what the author intended: his lifelong career in the theatre was a search for 'un style d'acteurs, débarrassés de ce faux naturel que nous devons au cinéma'. They may have twentieth-century settings and characters, and they may resemble, say, *Huis clos* and *Les Mains sales* respectively, but they need a different style of production.

One is reminded of Cocteau's famous *mot*: 'ce que le public te reproche, cultive-le. C'est toi.' It is a controversial formula for the development of the human personality which also points to the best way of putting Camus over in the theatre. Camus's plays are reproached (especially in the English and American theatre world as a result of bad, inept or casually naturalistic productions) with being 'eternal debates'. So let them be debates. Debates in which the philosophical implications are stressed and a high degree of tension is maintained. Sets should be minimal and stylized, lighting artificial and focused rather than natural. Gesture, movement and stage business likewise must be tightly controlled and sufficiently stylized to focus, punctuate and support the dialogue. A slackening of tension in mid-debate is fatal. Camus's dramatic style is the end of a long line of evolution: *Caligula* was written exactly 300 years after the first great French tragedy, Corneille's *Horace*. In a subtle and unspectacular way he has experimented with what the contemporary French *avant-garde* would consider to be a basically old-fashioned type of theatre to perfect and refine an articulate form for his ideas. The director's duty is to be faithful to these ideas, and this requires a considerable degree of artistic self-discipline. He must do everything possible to make his audience *listen*, for it is only this way, by being completely absorbed into the philosophical tension of the plays, that an audience can fully respond to the passion and originality of Camus's moral arguments. The author does not make the task easy. Unlike Anouilh, Giraudoux and Sartre, he does not provide any short cuts, either morally or artistically.

The real merit of Camus's theatre lies in the sphere of theme rather than form, in so far as it is possible to separate the success of one from the failure of the other. Camus's theatre constitutes the most sincere attempt in its genre to create philosophical theatre mirroring the metaphysical anguish of our age. At the same time it combats the nihilism to which such speculation can lead, and in this respect the author follows clearly in the tradition of the great French moralists. Camus's theatre is unequalled for the probity and passion with which it defended human values during a decade in France when they had never been more fragile.

Notes

Chapter 1

1. For Camus's remarks about these revivals 'generously stuffed with anachronisms', see John Cruickshank, *Albert Camus and the Literature of Revolt* (Oxford University Press, 1959), p. 192.
2. Cf. Interview in *TRN*, p. 1713.

Chapter 2

1. Camus's early unpublished 'adaptation' of *Prometheus Bound* is reported by Germaine Brée, who saw a manuscript of it in 1959, to have been faithful to the Aeschylus text with few modifications.
2. Technically Algeria was part of France; in effect, of course, it was a colony.
3. A. Durand, *Le Cas Albert Camus* (Fischbacher, 1961), pp. 39–40.
4. *Carnets* 1, p. 29.
5. A. Malraux, *Le Temps du mépris* (Gallimard, 1935), Preface, p. 8.
6. Quoted by F. Lumley, *Trends in Twentieth-Century Drama* (Barrie & Rockliff, 1960), p. 94.
7. Ibid., p. 95.
8. C. A. Viggiani, 'Albert Camus in 1936: the beginnings of a career', *Symposium*, XII (Spring-Fall 1958).

Chapter 3

1. See Walter Strauss, '*Caligula*: Ancient Sources and Modern Parallels', *Comparative Literature*, III, 2 (1951), p. 160, and John Cruickshank, *Albert Camus and the Literature of Revolt* (O.U.P., 1959), pp. 194-5.
2. C. Gadourek, *Les Innocents et les coupables: Essai d'exégèse de l'œuvre d'Albert Camus* (Mouton, 1963), p. 79.
3. Quoted in English translation by G. Brée, 'Camus' *Caligula*; Evolution of a Play', *Symposium*, XII (Spring-Fall 1958).
4. See particularly *Bulletins de l'Association Guillaume Budé* (Paris, 1964), 'Actes du 7e Congrès, Aix-en-Provence, 1963'.
5. *Les Îles* (Gallimard, 1958), p. 108, footnote.

6. Martin Esslin, *Brecht: A Choice of Evils* (Eyre & Spottiswoode, 1959), p. 113.

Chapter 4

1. D. M. Church, '*Le Malentendu:* Search for Modern Tragedy', *French Studies*, XX, 1 (January 1966), p. 35.

Chapter 5

1. J.-L. Barrault, *Réflexions sur le théâtre* (Vautrain, 1949), p. 60.
2. J. Guicharnaud, *Modern French Theatre* (Yale University Press, 1961), p. 230.
3. G. Marcel, 'Pourquoi l'Espagne?', *Les Nouvelles Littéraires* (11 Nov. 1948).
4. J. Lemarchand, in *Combat* (29 Oct. 1948).
5. R. Barjaval, in *Carrefour* (3 Nov. 1948).
6. P. Quemeneur, in *La Scène* (13 Nov. 1948).
7. R. Gay-Crosier, *Les Envers d'un échec: étude sur le théâtre d'Albert Camus* (Minard, 1967), p. 133.

Chapter 6

1. R. Quilliot, *La Mer et les prisons: Essai sur Albert Camus* (Gallimard, 1956), pp. 210–11.

Chapter 7

1. R. Poulet, 'Pourquoi adapte-t-il au lieu d'écrire? Voici le secret d'Albert Camus', *Carrefour* (25 Feb. 1959).
2. J. P. Couch, 'Camus' Dramatic Adaptations and Translations', *French Review*, 33, 1 (Oct. 1959).
3. R. Paseyro, 'Camus massacre Calderón', *Cahiers des Saisons*, 20 (1960).
4. R. Pignarre, *Histoire du théâtre* (Presses Universitaires de France, 1959), p. 63.
5. *Requiem for a Nun* (Penguin, 1960), pp. 130–1.
6. Quoted by D. Magarshack in Introduction to his translation of *The Devils* (Penguin, 1953).
7. *Les Démons*, trans. Boris de Schloezer (Pléiade, 1955), pp. 422–3.

Chapter 8

1. J. Guicharnaud, *Modern French Theatre* (Yale University Press, 1961), p. 132.
2. T. Bishop, *Pirandello and the French Theatre* (New York University Press, 1961), p. 129.
3. J. N. Maféi, in *Nouvelle Jeunesse* (1 Dec. 1944).
4. Martin Esslin, *The Theatre of the Absurd* (Eyre & Spottiswoode, 1962; rev. 1968), Introduction.

Bibliography

An enormous number of books and articles have been devoted to various aspects of Camus's work. This bibliography is necessarily selective (particularly the article section).

1 Bibliographies

BOLLINGER, R. *Albert Camus. Eine Bibliographie über ihn und sein Werk.* Cologne, Greven Verlag, 1957.

CRÉPIN, S. *Albert Camus. Essai de bibliographie.* Brussels, Commission belge de bibliographie, 1960.

FITCH, B. *Essai de bibliographie des études en langue française consacrées à Albert Camus, 1937–1962.* Calepins de bibliographie. Paris, Minard, 1965.

HOY, P. *Camus in English. An annotated bibliography of Albert Camus's contributions to English and American periodicals and newspapers.* Wymondham, Melton Mowbray, Brewhouse Press, 1968.

ROEMING. R. F. *Camus: a Bibliography.* Madison–London, University of Wisconsin Press, 1968.

2 Books specifically on Camus

ALBÉRÈS, R.-M. (ed.). *Camus.* (Essays by M. Lebesque [on Camus's theatre], P. de Boisdeffre, J. Daniel, P. Gascar, A. Parinaud, E. Roblès, J. Roy, P.-H. Simon.) Paris, Hachette, 1964.

BONNIER, H. *Albert Camus ou la force d'être.* Lyons and Paris, Vitte, 1959.

BRÉE, G. *Camus.* Rutgers University Press, 1959. Revised edn. New York, Harcourt, Brace, 1964.

BRÉE, G. (ed.) *Camus: a Collection of Critical Essays.* New Jersey, Prentice-Hall, 1962.

BRISVILLE, J.-C. *Camus.* Paris, Gallimard, 1959.

CHAMPIGNY, R. *Sur un héros païen.* Paris, Gallimard, 1959.

COOMBS, I. *Camus, homme de théâtre.* Paris, Nizet, 1968.

CRUICKSHANK, J. *Albert Camus and the Literature of Revolt*. London, Oxford University Press, 1959.

DURAND, A. *Le Cas Albert Camus*. Paris, Fischbacher, 1961.

GADOUREK, C. *Les Innocents et les coupables: Essai d'exégèse de l'œuvre d'Albert Camus*. The Hague, Mouton, 1963.

GAY-CROSIER, R. *Les Envers d'un échec: étude sur le théâtre d'Albert Camus*. Paris, Minard, 1967.

GÉLINAS, G.-P. *La Liberté dans la pensée d'Albert Camus*. Fribourg, Éditions Universitaires, 1965.

GINESTIER, P. *La Pensée de Camus*. Paris, Bordas, 1964.

GRENIER, J. *Albert Camus (Souvenirs)*. Paris, Gallimard, 1968.

HAGGIS, D. R. *Camus: La Peste*. London, Edward Arnold, 1962.

HANNA, T. *The Thought and Art of Albert Camus*. Chicago, Henry Regnery Company, 1958.

HOURDIN, G. *Camus le juste*. Paris, Cerf, 1960.

KING, A. *Camus*. Edinburgh and London, Oliver and Boyd, 1964.

LEBESQUE, M. *Camus par lui-même*. Paris, du Seuil, 1963.

LUPPÉ, R. DE. *Albert Camus*. Paris, Éditions Universitaires, 1952.

MAJAULT, J. *Camus, révolte et liberté*. Paris, Centurion, 1965.

MAQUET, A. *Albert Camus ou l'invincible été*. Paris, Debresse, 1956.

MATTHEWS, J. H. (ed.). *Camus devant la critique anglo-saxonne*. Paris, Minard, 1961.

NGUYEN-VAN-HUY, P. *La Métaphysique du bonheur chez Albert Camus*. Neuchâtel, La Baconnière, 1962.

ONIMUS, J. *Camus*. Les Écrivains devant Dieu. Paris, Desclée de Brouwer, 1965.

PARKER, E. *Albert Camus, the Artist in the Arena*. University of Wisconsin Press, 1965.

PINNOY, M. *Albert Camus*. Paris, Desclée de Brouwer, 1961.

QUILLIOT, R. *La Mer et les prisons: Essai sur Albert Camus*. Paris, Gallimard, 1956.

SCOTT, N. A. *Albert Camus*. London, Bowes & Bowes, 1962.

SIMON, P.-H. *Présence de Camus*. Brussels, Renaissance du Livre, 1961.

THIEBERGER, R. (ed.). *Camus devant la critique de langue allemande*. Paris, Minard, 1963.

THODY, P. *Albert Camus, 1913–1960*. London, Hamish Hamilton, 1961.

THOORENS, L. *Albert Camus*. Paris, La Sixaine, 1946.

3 Articles

ABRAHAM, C. *Caligula*, Drama of Revolt or Drama of Deception? *Modern Drama*, V, 4, February 1963.

ALTER, A. De *Caligula* aux *Justes*. *Revue d'Histoire du Théâtre*, IV, Oct.–Dec. 1960.

ARTAUD, A. Lettre à Albert Camus. *Nouvelle Revue Française*, May 1960.

BARRAULT, J.-L. Sur *L'État de siège*. *La Table Ronde*, February 1960.

BEHRENS, R. Existential 'Character-Ideas' in Camus's *The Misunderstanding*. *Modern Drama* VII, 2, September 1964.

BESPALOFF, R. Le Monde du condamné à mort. *Esprit*, XVIII, January 1950.

BRÉE, G. Albert Camus and the 'Théâtre de l'Équipe'. *French Review*, 3, January 1949.

— *Caligula*, Evolution of a Play. *Symposium*, XII, 1958.

CASTEX, P.-G. Les Contradictions d'Albert Camus. *Le Français dans le monde*, September 1966.

CHARLESWORTH, M. P. The Tradition about Caligula. *Cambridge Historical Journal*, IV, 2, 1933.

CHURCH, D. M. *Le Malentendu:* Search for Modern Tragedy. *French Studies*, XX, 1, January 1966.

CLAYTON, A. J. Note sur Camus et Suétone: La source ancienne de deux passages des *Carnets*. *French Studies*, XX, 2, April 1966.

COUCH, J. P. Camus' Dramatic Adaptations and Translations. *French Review*, XXXIII, 1, October 1959.

— Camus and Faulkner. *Yale French Studies*, XXV, 1960.

DURÁN, M. Camus and the Spanish Theatre. *Yale French Studies*, XXV, Spring 1960.

FARABET, R. Albert Camus à l'avant-scène. *Revue d'Histoire du Théâtre*, IV, 1960.

FREEMAN, E. Camus' Brechtian Apprenticeship in the Theatre. *Forum for Modern Language Studies*, IV, 3, July 1968.

— Camus, Suetonius, and the Caligula Myth. *Symposium*, XXIV, 3, Fall 1970.

— *Les Justes* – Modern Tragedy or Old-Fashioned Melodrama? *Modern Language Quarterly*, 31, 1, March 1970.

GOURFINKEL, N. *Les Possédés*. *Revue d'Histoire du Théâtre*, Oct.–Dec. 1960.

HOWARTH, W. D. History in the Theatre: the French and English Traditions. *Trivium*, I, 1966.

JEANSON, F. Pirandello et Camus, à travers *Henri IV* et *Caligula*. *Les Temps Modernes*, 61, Nov. 1950.

LEBESQUE, M. La Passion pour la scène, in R.-M. Albérès (ed.), *Camus*. Paris, Hachette, 1964.

LERMINIER, G. Brecht et Camus. *L'Âge Nouveau*, XII, Jan. 1957.

MCPHEETERS, D. W. Camus' translations of Lope and Calderón. *Symposium*, XII, 1958.

MELCHINGER, S. Les Éléments baroques dans le théâtre de Camus, in R. Thieberger (ed.), *Camus devant la critique de langue allemande*. Paris, Minard, 1963.

MINON, J.-M. Sources et remaniements du *Caligula* de Camus. *Revue de l'Université de Bruxelles*, 12, 1959–60.

NÉGRONI, J. Albert Camus et le Théâtre de l'Équipe. *Revue d'Histoire du Théâtre*, Oct.-Dec. 1960.

NORTH, R. J. Myth in the Modern French Theatre. University of Keele Publications, 1962.

ONIMUS, J. Camus adapte à la scène Faulkner et Dostoïevski. *Revue des Sciences Humaines*, Oct.-Dec. 1961.

PASEYRO, R. Camus massacre Calderón. *Les Cahiers des Saisons*, 20, 1960.

POULET, R. Pourquoi adapte-t-il au lieu d'écrire? Voici le secret d'Albert Camus. *Carrefour*, 25, February 1959.

RECK, R. D. The Theatre of Albert Camus. *Modern Drama*, 4, 1, May 1961.

SAVAGE, E. B. Masks and Mummeries in *Enrico IV* and *Caligula*. *Modern Drama*, 6, 4, February 1964.

SONNENFELD, A. Albert Camus as Dramatist: the sources of his failure. *Tulane Drama Review*, Summer 1961.

STRAUSS, W. A. *Caligula*: ancient sources and modern parallels. *Comparative Literature*, III, 2, Spring 1951.

VIGGIANI, C. A. Albert Camus in 1936: the beginnings of a career. *Symposium*, XII, Spring-Fall 1958.

VILAR, J. Camus régisseur. *Nouvelle Revue Française*, 87, 1960.

VIRTANEN, R. Camus' *Le Malentendu* and some Analogues. *Comparative Literature*, X, 3, Summer 1958.

WALKER, I. H. The Composition of *Caligula*. *Symposium*, XX, 3, Fall 1966.

Many of the articles listed above, plus scores of others about Camus but not necessarily pertaining to his plays, are to be found in special issues of magazines and journals of which the following are the most useful:

Le Figaro Littéraire, 9 January 1960.
La Nouvelle Revue Française, 87, March 1960.
Revue d'Histoire du Théâtre, XII, 4, Oct.–Dec. 1960.
Symposium, XII, 1–2, Spring–Fall 1958.
Symposium, XXIV, 3, Fall 1970.
La Table Ronde, 146, February 1960.
Simoun, 32, July 1960.
Yale French Studies, 25, Spring, 1960.

Finally, an extremely valuable source of a different nature is the 'Fonds Rondel' in the Bibliothèque de l'Arsenal, Paris. This is a collection of theatre programmes, and press cuttings concerning the productions of Camus's plays: previews, interviews, cartoons, photographs and critical reviews.

4 General Background

ALBÉRÈS, R.-M. *La Révolte des écrivains d'aujourd'hui*. Paris, Corrêa, 1949.

AMBRIÈRE, F. *Le Théâtre français depuis la Libération*. Paris, Corrêa, 1949.

ARTAUD, A. *Le Théâtre et son double*. Paris, Gallimard, 1964.

AYLEN, L. *Greek Tragedy and the Modern World*. London, Methuen, 1964.

BARNES, H. E. *The Literature of Possibility – A Study in Humanistic Existentialism*. London, Tavistock, 1961.

BARRAULT, J.-L., and RENAUD, M. *Antonin Artaud et le théâtre de notre temps*. Paris, Julliard, 1958.

BEIGBEDER, M. *Le Théâtre en France depuis la Libération*. Paris, Bordas, 1959.

BENTLEY, E. *The Playwright as Thinker*. New York, Harcourt, Brace, 1946.

BISHOP, T. *Pirandello and the French Theatre*. New York University Press, 1960.

CURTIS, A. *New Developments in the French Theatre*. London, Curtain Press, 1948.

ESSLIN, M. *The Theatre of the Absurd*. London, Eyre & Spottiswoode, 1962, revised 1968.

FERGUSSON, F. *The Idea of a Theatre*. Princeton University Press, 1949.

FOWLIE, W. *Dionysus in Paris - A Guide to Contemporary French Theatre*. London, Gollancz, 1961.

GASCOIGNE, B. *Twentieth-Century Drama*. London, Hutchinson, 1962.

GASSNER, J. *Form and Idea in the Modern Theatre*. New York, Holt, Rinehart and Winston, 1956.

GOUHIER, H. *L'Essence du théâtre*. Paris, Plon, 1943.

GROSSVOGEL, D. I. *Twentieth-Century French Drama*. Columbia University Press, 1961.

GUICHARNAUD, J. *Modern French Theatre from Giraudoux to Beckett*. Yale University Press, 1961.

HINCHCLIFFE, A. P. *The Absurd*. London, Methuen, 1969.

KEMP, R. *La Vie du théâtre*. Paris, Albin Michel, 1956.

LALOU, R. *Le Théâtre en France depuis 1900*. Paris, Presses Universitaires de France, 1951.

LUMLEY, F. *Trends in Twentieth-Century Drama*. London, Barrie & Rockliff, 1960.

PRONKO, L. C. *Avant-Garde: The Experimental Theater in France*. Cambridge University Press, 1962.

SIMON, P.-H. *Théâtre et destin*. Paris, Armand Colin, 1959.

STEINER, G. *The Death of Tragedy*. London, Faber & Faber, 1961.

STYAN, J. L. *The Dark Comedy*. Cambridge University Press, 1962, revised 1968.

WILLIAMS, R. *Modern Tragedy*. London, Chatto and Windus, 1966.

Index